A TO Z OF SCIENCE

Basher Science™

A TO Z OF SCIENCE

A VISUAL DICTIONARY FOR CURIOUS SCIENTISTS

AMPLITUDE

ION

HEART

KINGFISHER

LONDON & NEW YORK

KINGFISHER
LONDON & NEW YORK

Text copyright © Toucan Books Ltd. 2019, 2021
Based on an original concept by Toucan Books Ltd.
Illustrations copyright © Simon Basher 2019, 2021
Designed and created by Basher
www.basherscience.com

First published in 2019
This edition published in 2021 in the United States by Kingfisher
120 Broadway, New York, NY 10271
Kingfisher is an imprint of Macmillan Children's Books, London

Simon Basher would like to dedicate this book to everyone that has
supported the Basher Science series.
In memory of William "Bill" Penn (1937-2018)

Author: Tom Jackson (with Dan Green and Adrian Dingle)
Consultant: Dr. Mike Goldsmith
Editor: Anna Southgate
Indexer: Marie Lorimer

Distributed in the U.S. and Canada by Macmillan,
120 Broadway, New York, NY 10271

Library of Congress Cataloging-in-Publication Data
has been applied for

ISBN 978-0-7534-7420-4 (HB)
       978-0-7534-7421-1 (PB)

Kingfisher books are available for special promotions and premiums.
For details contact: Special Markets Department, Macmillan,
120 Broadway, New York, NY 10271.

For more information, please visit www.kingfisherbooks.com

Printed in China

9 8 7 6 5 4 3 2 1
1TR/0721/WKT/UG/128MA

EU representative: Macmillan Publishers Ireland Limited, Mallard Lodge,
Lansdowne Village, Dublin 4

CONTENTS

A

▽ Acid

I'm mad, bad, often smelly, and dangerous to know. Given half the chance, I'll eat away at Metal and burn through Skin! What gives me my acidic nature is my ability to lose hydrogen ions. I'm a sinister splitter: in the presence of Water, I disassociate, breaking into a negative ion and a positive hydrogen ion (H^+)—a little fellow called a spare proton (I'm sometimes called a "proton donor"). Sparky Hydrogen is now free to react with other chemicals in the area and can create ten kinds of havoc!

Really strong acids instantly lose 100 percent of their H^+ ions, while weak acids hold them closer for longer. Super-strong sulfuric acid is number one in the chemical industry; weak acetic acid is number one when sprinkled on your salad as vinegar.

▷ Absolute Zero

How low can you go? Not as low as I can, that's for sure. I am the coldest that Temperature can get, about −460°F (−273°C). That's colder than outer space.

▷ Acceleration

I've got what it takes to get you going. I'm an increase in speed, and I happen when Force acts on Mass. Thanks to me, you get faster with each beat of time.

■ Acid Rain

I form when Pollution in Air mixes with raindrops. I'm a harsh chemical rain that can eat away at stone, kill trees, and change the acidity of soil and River.

▷ Acoustics

I'm the science of sound. Did you hear that? The science of sound! I track the passage of Sound's waves and can explain the way Ear hears things. I'm also used for making and recording music. People even find me handy when they want to soundproof something for a little peace and quiet.

■ Acre

How big is that forest over there? How about the neighbor's farm? I'm the unit of measure you'll need. There are about 640 of me in a square mile (247 of me in a square kilometer).

■ Action and Reaction

The great English scientist Sir Isaac Newton introduced us to the world in his Laws of Motion, which say that every action has an equal and opposite reaction. He was being polite. We say that if you push something (that's Action), prepare for a simultaneous push in return (that's Reaction). We are created when Force meets Mass, and we help explain why it takes effort to get things moving. Rocket relies on us entirely. The downward blast of Rocket's engine makes Action, and so Reaction pushes upward.

▽ Activation Energy

It takes some oomph to get Chemical Reaction going, and I am the minimum energy required. Some reactions, such as when Hydrogen bonds with Oxygen to make Water, need only a tiny push to get going, Luckily for you, most reactions need a lot more. If you've ever watched a novice trying to light a fire—angry, cold, and getting tired out—you'll know that wood and coal need more than a little spark to burst into flames.

It's not only Combustion who needs my kick. Chemists often heat up chemicals to make them react faster in the lab. The extra energy breaks open the stable chemical bonds in a mixture, and that allows the chemicals to reorganize into new substances. Activation energy can be provided by Light, Pressure, and even Sound, as well as Heat.

A

▷ Active Site

Enzyme will tell you that it has a very specific job to do, and I'm the place to get it done. You see, Enzyme's molecule has a special shape. I'm the part of that shape that grabs hold of Reactant so that Enzyme can accelerate its chemical conversion into Product.

▷ Aerobe

Work it, baby! I'm a bacterium that thrives in Atmosphere when it is rich with Oxygen. Aerobic bacteria use that powerful gas to split (oxidize) Molecule, which can be sugar or fat. This releases Energy, usually with Carbon Dioxide and Water. It's a trick that Cell does in almost all living creatures.

A

■ Aerodynamic

Built to slide through Air, I'm the streamlined shape of planes, cars, Rocket, and Bird. I allow these things to move easily without Air piling up in front and getting in the way.

■ Aerosol

I'm a mysterious mist of Liquid or Solid floating in Gas. I'm often released from spray cans and particles are made in Atmosphere, but I exist in nature, too. Pollen, Salt, and Bacterium are all floating in Air as versions of me.

▽ Air

Breathe me in, I'm all you've got. I'm all around you, but you won't see me—unless you look up, perhaps. I'm an invisible mixture of colorless gases. I'm mostly made from Nitrogen (78 percent) and Oxygen (21 percent). About 1 percent is Argon, and a tiny bit (about 0.04 percent) is Carbon Dioxide. Oxygen is the most important, which is why you breathe me in. I also have a varying volume of water vapor. When the amount gets too high, Water falls out as rain.

I'm completely see-through at night. Look up at me in the daytime, though, and I appear blue. Sky blue to be exact. That is because, as Sun's light shines in from space, the blue light takes an indirect route, bouncing from one part of the sky to another, before finally reaching your eyes.

■ Air Pressure

I ain't heavy, but I'm always pushing against you. One way to think of me is to consider Air's weight. All that gas in a tall column above you is pushing down the whole time. No one feels anything—you're used to it—but every square inch of Skin has a weight of about 15 lb. squeezing it at any one time (1 kg per square cm). That's at sea level, and I reduce the higher you go, where there is less Air above pushing down. Atop the peak of Mount Everest, I'm only one-third as strong.

■ Air Resistance

Sometimes called drag, I'm the force of Air pushing back on objects as they try to move. My strength grows with the size of the object and its speed. Engineers make things aerodynamic to keep me to a minimum.

▷ Alcohol

Many folk find me intoxicating company, but be careful, because I can bite hard. As Ethanol—the active ingredient in alcoholic drinks—I am the world's most notorious depressant. Scratch my glitzy surface too much, and you will find a drab, sad existence. As a group of chemicals, however, I'm so much more. For example, the alcohol glycol stays gloopy at very low temperatures, making it a handy antifreeze.

In me, Molecule is nothing more complicated than Hydrocarbon with one or more attached OH groups. With my polar OH group (Covalent Bond with positive and negative ends), I make Solvent, which is very good at dissolving Solid. "Gasohol," a mixture of petroleum and Ethanol that's used as fuel, is produced from sugar cane.

▷ Alga

I live just like a plant. I make my own food from Light, thanks to Photosynthesis. Look closely and you will see that, in most cases, my body is made up of just one cell. I like to bundle together in clumps, but I can survive well enough all by myself. I'm most commonly found in Water, floating around as Plankton.

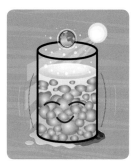

■ Alimentary Canal

I'm the proper name for your guts, the food tube made by Stomach and Intestines that runs through your body from your mouth all the way to your rear end.

A

▷ Alkali

I'm a type of chemical that always goes on the attack whenever I come across Acid. There is never a winner between us—we fight to the death, leaving nothing but Water and some salty leftovers. I'm a kind of base chemical—the most powerful Base there is—and one that can dissolve in Water.

■ Alkali Metal

I am a kind of soft and shiny metal, such as Potassium. I burn fiercely, making colorful flames, and when I react with Water, I form a type of alkali.

A

▷ Allele

Pronounced AL-EEL, I'm a tricky character to understand, so listen up. You'll have heard about genes, perhaps? Well, Gene codes a trait that you inherit from your mom and dad. That's where I come in. You receive two of each gene—one from each parent. Each version is an allele, which is me. Hello! Every gene has several different alleles. For example, Gene controls Eye's color, and there are alleles for green, brown, and blue.

All people have the same set of genes, but a different collection of alleles. That is what makes them unique. Alleles fight it out to decide what characteristic you end up with. Sometimes, one of us is dominant and gets to decide; other times, a group of us team up to work together.

■ Allergy

I don't want to be inappropriate, but I can't help it. I'm what happens when Immune System goes wrong and launches an attack on something harmless. That harmless thing is called an allergen. For example, tiny Pollen is a common allergen floating in Air. It causes a form of allergy called hay fever, which makes you sneeze and have itchy eyes. Most types of me are annoying yet harmless, but sometimes I can be deadly. Doctors help to keep me under control, but no one really knows where I come from.

■ Allotrope

Element is a simple kind of guy but can appear in more than one form—that's me. For example, diamond and graphite are both allotropes of Carbon.

▷ Alloy

A human-made version of Metal, I put a little "steel" into softer types. I'm made by melting two metals, and sometimes other elements, and mixing them together. That mix of differently sized atoms locks together well and gives more of a backbone to spineless metals. So I'm harder, tougher, and less flexible than pure Metal. I give metals properties that better suit their uses. I blend Carbon and Iron to make super-strong Steel. Adding chromium to the mix stops rust from forming and makes Steel stainless. Copper and Tin combine to make tough bronze, while Copper and Zinc make shiny brass.

■ Almanac

If you need to know some important information, turn to me. I started out as a little book printed afresh each year—but could be an app or website today—and I hold information about the coming year. Want to know Tide's timing, when Sun rises and sets, or the position of bright Star day by day? Just ask me, I'm here to help.

▷ Alpha Centauri

As the closest star to Sun, I look like a single light, but I'm actually three in one. Alpha Centauri A is a little bigger than Sun, while Alpha Centauri B is a little smaller, and our combined light makes us the third-brightest star in the sky. Our third member, tiny Proxima Centauri, is the closest of us to Sun, although it is hard to see.

A

▷ Alpha Particle

In the teeny world of subatomic particles, I am a big bruiser. I'm a chunky mix of two protons and two neutrons, and I'm not to be messed with— steer clear of me. When I get into your body, I plow into chemicals, wrecking Cell and causing cancers. Luckily for you, just a few layers of Skin is enough to stop me.

■ Alternating Current

I'm an electric current that is always changing direction—50 or 60 times a second. I'm easier to make and travel more efficiently than my straightforward friend Direct Current.

▷ Aluminum

I'm light on my feet, and my pocket-battleship strength has made me a powerhouse metal. I'm a featherweight who literally punches above my weight! I offer a blend of strength and lightness—you can make me into planes, soda cans, and foil. I am the third-most abundant element in Earth's rocks—and one of Metal's most common forms—but you must work hard to see me and even harder to make me pure. Extracting me from my ore, bauxite, takes a huge amount of electrical power.

Once pure, I'm very easy to recycle—make sure that you do that! My salts help purify Water by turning suspended impurities into solids that sink harmlessly to the bottom. However, I'm poisonous in large amounts and can even turn Hair green!

A

▷ Amber

I'm hard but smooth and look like I have sunlight locked inside me, preserved forever. I've been used in jewelry since the Stone Age, but I'm no stone. I get my golden glow by starting out as sticky resin that oozed from trees. Then I toughened up—slowly. I look like new, but I'm millions of years old.

■ Amino Acid

I'm a simple chemical soul with Nitrogen at my heart. When I get together in a long chain, I form Protein, which is among the most complicated natural chemicals of all.

■ Amoeba

"You better shape up!" they said. I said, "No, no, no." I'm a single-celled critter that takes many forms. I am changing shape all the time, as my insides flow in one direction dragging the rest of me along. I can also extend to create armlike extensions to grab hold of food or a surface. I'm normally a good guy but can be bad. It is me that causes nasty illnesses like dysentery.

■ Ampere

I took my name from the French scientist André-Marie Ampère, but people know me best as amp. I'm Electric Current's unit, and I'm used to measure Charge's motion. Roughly speaking, one of me (1 A) adds up to six million trillion electrons moving through a wire every second.

▷ Amphibian

I belong to a group of secretive, sun-shy creatures. Get to know us and you'll love us, warts and all! Besides leaping frogs and waddling toads, we include salamanders, newts, and rarely seen legless weirdos called caecilians. (They are blind, so they don't see you either.) We live in damp places because we breathe through our skin and need to keep it moist and fresh.

We were the first vertebrates to try life on land, 400 million years ago. Since then, we've been commuting between land and water. Some of us never leave the water even now, and our fishy past is there for all to see in the jelly-covered eggs we lay, always in or close to water. Born with gills, our babies spend their childhood in water. Once they grow lungs, they can hunt on land.

A

▷ Amplitude

I'm the measure of Wave's height, taken from its midpoint and up to its crest (or down to its trough). I can be used to describe any wave. With water waves, the higher the wave is, the more energy it carries and the bigger it breaks. In the case of Sound, increasing me makes Wave louder, and with Light, it's me that boosts brightness.

▷ Anaerobe

I'm a bacterial garbageman and a noxious, bubbling bottom feeder. I can live without Oxygen and so pop up in places where other life stays away. Without me, you would soon be choking on your own waste. Animals can go anaerobic if they need to, and run without Oxygen for a short time. It makes them very tired and out of breath.

■ Anabolic Steroid

A steroid is a chemical signal used in animal bodies, and anabolic means "build." My job is to make a body grow.

▽ Analog

I'm a scratchy old dude, but I make no apologies. I have had a long and illustrious career in broadcasting, but sadly the modern world chooses fashionable Digital over me. Nevertheless, I remain a specialist—and I'm not without advantages. I am the original way of sending information from one place to another. The trick is to encode information onto "carrier waves," such as Radio Wave or changing Electric Current. This new, "modulated" wave has peaks and troughs that mirror the original message. It can be decoded to extract the info, but parts of the wave often go missing.

My first use was in telephones. Later came radio, TV, and vinyl records. These days, most people listen to Digital's music, but many still love me for my quirks.

A

■ Anatomy

I'm the branch of Biology that studies the form of living bodies. As well as checking out the outside, I'll take a good look inside a body.

■ Anesthetic

Just relax, you won't feel a thing—thanks to me. I'm a drug used by doctors to stop the body from feeling anything during surgery.

■ Angle

Unless two infinite straight lines are parallel, they always cross one another, and you'll find me where they meet. I loiter at the corners of geometrical shapes. When I am acute, I am tight, sharp, and less than 90°. Obtuse means I am between 90° and 180°. A straight line has an angle of 180°, a right angle is 90° exactly, and a reflex angle can be anywhere from 180° to 360°.

■ Anion

I occur when Atom gains Electron (or two, or three). That extra charge makes me a negative ion. Most anions are nonmetals. I am deeply attracted to my opposite, Cation. It's an attraction that creates a strong chemical bond between us.

▷ Anode

A battery's plus sign, I'm the positive part that connects to Circuit so that Electric Current can get on the move. Negative Anion is always being pulled toward me.

■ Antenna

I have two forms. The first involves the feelers on a critter's head—Insect has them. These do sometimes work by feeling around, but they are more often scent detectors. Second, I'm the transmitter or receiver for a radio, router, phone, or other techno gadget that picks up invisible signal waves. Do you receive my double meaning?

▷ Antibiotic

Before I came along, almost everyone who got a bad infection died. But I'm built to be Bacterium's killer. I'm a magic drug that kills the bacteria making you sick while leaving the rest of you alone. My first appearance was as penicillin, a medicine made from mold. Today, Superbug has learned to resist me, and the search is on to make new types.

■ Antibody

We are bug busters that cruise through Blood's highways on the lookout for intruders. When we find 'em, we waste 'em in a hail of protein-jacketed ammo. Each one of us is built to lock on to one particular Virus or other bad guy. Then we call in Immune System to waste those suckers.

■ Antigen

Hey, look at me! I'm a marker chemical on Cell's surface. I'm there to tell Immune System that I belong to the body—and Antibody searches me out to spot germs.

▽ Antimatter

Did you think I was mere science fiction? Think again! I'm science *fact*, baby, and you'd better get wise to me! I am Matter's evil twin and the nemesis of every Atom in your body. When my dark, mirror-image Antiparticle comes into contact with Matter's particles, they mutually destroy each other in a flash of raw energy. All of my mass is transferred instantly into super-energetic Gamma Ray—a return on investment unheard of in the energy generation game, making me about 10 billion times more powerful than burning oil.

A half-gram of me could set off a Hiroshima-size blast. I'm just the ticket to power spacecraft to the stars, but I'm hard to make, and with a talent for Matter's destruction, I'm devilishly tricky to store.

A

▷ Antiparticle

An evil twin, I have an identical mass to Particle, but the opposite charge. I am created in high-energy collisions. Whenever I meet Matter, the result is a flash of pure Energy.

Shake hands with your antimatter twin, and you'd both be destroyed in a catastrophic nuclear explosion!

■ Antiseptic

As a cream, powder, or liquid, I am here to help. My role is to kill the tiny germs in a fresh cut before they can multiply to a damaging and dangerous level.

A

■ Arch

An *arch*-itectural wonder, I am an ancient structure whose curved upper part takes the weight pushing down from above and channels it sideways down strong sturdy legs.

▷ Archaea

Don't listen to Bacterium—we were here first! We hang out in the deepest rocks and oceans, we chill out inside nuclear waste tanks. We thrive in hot mud, salt lakes, and deadly Acid. We can endure icy cold and crushing Pressure. Some of us obtain Energy from sunlight, while others live in animal guts, helping cows digest grass. We are also handy in sewage treatment. It is from us toughies that scientists get useful enzymes that can withstand Heat, Acid, and Alkali. And, unlike some bacteria, we don't cause disease!

■ Archimedes (c. 287–212 B.C.E.)

The great-granddaddy of all inventors was ancient Greek Archimedes, the original gadget geek. He just couldn't stop inventing great gizmos. The Archimedes' screw is still used to lift Water and is the guiding principle behind a ship's propeller. His "death ray" used mirrors to concentrate Sun's energy onto Roman ships, while a giant claw tipped them over so they sank!

Archimedes was also a mathematician and worked on number puzzles. He calculated the number *pi* accurately by working out the perimeter (distance around the edge) of almost round shapes with more than 90 sides. Next, he tried to figure out the number of sand grains that would fill Universe. He was way out but invented a way to handle large numbers in the process.

▷ Area

I'll tell you the exact size of any shape you want, using any square unit you like. Take a flat shape, for example. A line has one dimension (length) and a flat shape has two

dimensions (length plus width). I measure the space within these dimensions by multiplying one by the other. For a three-dimensional shape, you'll need my friend Volume.

▷ Argon

Completely idle and basically lazy, I'm totally lackluster—an odorless, colorless, and tasteless Gas. Wild argon is renowned for its inability to react with anything, but this can

be a good thing. I am used as an "inert atmosphere" in potentially dangerous jobs, such as arc welding, when Oxygen must be excluded in order to avoid explosions.

■ Aristotle (384–322 B.C.E.)

Philosophers are smart; Aristotle was a philosopher; Aristotle was smart. Logical, isn't it? Greek genius Aristotle was one of the very first scientists. He believed only what he could see, and he used that to explain things. But he was almost always wrong. For example, he thought Earth was built from layers of Rock, Water, Air, and Fire, and that Star hung inside a crystal sphere.

■ Arithmetic

Easy as 1 + 2, I'm the basic parts of mathematics—things like adding and multiplying. When a set of numbers grows arithmetically, it means each number gets bigger by adding to it. Each increase matches the last one. Data can also grow geometrically, which involves multiplying the numbers—so they grow by more each time.

▽ Arsenic

Make no mistake, I am a deadly element, and a master of disguise, too! One minute I'm gray Metal, the next I'm yellow-colored Nonmetal. I wreak havoc in developing countries where industrial Pollution allows me to sneak into the drinking water. Contamination with me causes widespread health issues. Nasty!

A

▷ Artery

Operating a large part of Circulatory System, I run the mainline expressways that lead away from Heart. My precious cargo is mostly bright-red, oxygen-carrying Blood (my pulmonary branch line delivers oxygen-poor Blood to the lungs). Heart pumps Blood under tremendous pressure, and I need thick, meaty walls to keep it contained.

■ Arthritis

Ouch, I hurt! I'm a common problem where Bone's joint becomes damaged, making it swell up and become stiff and sore.

A

▷ Arthropod

Welcome to the age of the arthropod! More than 84 percent of all animals on this planet belong in my mind-boggling Invertebrate collection. We arthropods rule this planet. We evolved from Worm somewhere out there on the seabed more than half a billion years ago. Our name means "jointed legs," and we've got a lot of them. Our most common member is Insect, with a measly six limbs, but scuttling millipedes have 200-plus!

I have a body formed in sections. Unlike Vertebrate, which hangs its squidgy parts on an internal skeleton, I keep my soft pieces safe in a suit of armor called an exoskeleton. Our Antennae pals—feelers—do more than feel; they help us smell, too. We see the world differently from you. A spider has up to eight eyes, don't you know!

▷ Artificial Intelligence

Beep, beep. I'm a new kind of computer program that's designed to make tough decisions. I'm still relatively young, and my first real job is to suggest products and ads you might like on the Internet. When I grow up, I hope to work on big, complex projects, such as designing new road layouts or laying cables under a city.

■ Artificial Selection

Farmers choose to breed strong or special plants and animals to create more useful types for eating or working, or as pets.

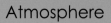

■ Asexual Reproduction

Reproduction is the way new living things are made. Often it requires two parents, a mom and a dad, but not always—sometimes a mom is all you need. I'm the name for this one-parent system, and I'm used by most kinds of animal, (some of the time), but never Mammal. Plants such as strawberries spread using me, too. By doing away with dads, I remove the chance to mix things up. Young made my way are identical to their mom. I allow one parent to fill the land with young quickly, but without variation they are at risk from diseases.

■ Asterism

I'm the smaller friend of Constellation. Instead of large patterns of stars, I'm just shapes made with the brighter ones.

▷ Asteroid

An irregular-shaped piece of space rock, I jostle with my pals around an elliptical path, forming a gappy "belt" that separates the inner planets and the gas giant gang. Jupiter's bullying gravitational pull has shepherded us into this no-man's-land.

Jupiter works with Gravity to make us crash into one another and shatter, so we've never been able to join together to form a planet. Once in a while, Jupiter's gravity flings one of us into a wider, more erratic orbit or sucks one of us into that of Jupiter.

Some of us, called near-Earth asteroids (NEAs), are "nasty 'roids," whose orbits could send them tumbling on a course dangerously close to Earth. So, watch out, there are asteroids about!

■ Astronomical Unit

I keep things simple for astronomers. I am the distance from Earth to Sun, and that's a useful unit for measuring space.

▷ Atmosphere

Think of me as a gassy blanket wrapped around a planet, held in place by Gravity. In Earth's case, I soak up Sun's nasty rays and trap Heat to keep things cozy down where you are.

Weather plays around in my troposphere. Above that, Ozone has its own layer in my stratosphere. Beyond that, I get really thin as I begin to merge with space.

A

▽ Atom

I am all around you—every object you pick up or sit on is made of me, even the air you breathe. In your body, Skin, Bone, and Blood are all made from me. I'm so small, you could hide trillions of me behind a single human hair with room to spare. No wonder it took scientists 2,000 years to track me down!

I fit a lot of heft inside me, but mostly I'm empty space. Protons and neutrons squeeze into my tiny central "nucleus," and electrons orbit around it. I'm quite happy to lose or gain electrons in chemical reactions with other atoms. To break me open is easy—you do it every time you switch on the TV—but splitting Nucleus is ridiculously hard and requires a great deal of energy. This is why atoms made at the beginning of time are still around today. I'm gonna live forever!

A

■ Atomic Energy
See **Nuclear Energy**

■ Atomic Mass

Although Atom is always made using the same set of building blocks, not all atoms are the same—and I'm here to help figure out the difference. An atom's nucleus can have anywhere from one to 200 or more particles in it. Those protons, neutrons, and electrons add up to give Atom a mass, and every element has atoms with a unique mass value. For example, Hydrogen's atomic mass is 1, while Oxygen's is 8.

■ Atomic Number

I'm the simplest way to understand the difference between atoms: I'm the number of protons in a nucleus. Every element has a unique atomic number and atomic properties that go with it. That is what makes them different from each other.

■ Atrium

There are two of me, one on each side at the top of Heart. We are the smaller chambers that receive Blood coming in. Bigger, stronger ventricles then pump it out.

■ Aurora

Move over, fireworks—I'm the ultimate light show. My full name is the *aurora borealis*, or northern lights. I can be *aurora australis*, which means southern lights, as well, but fewer people are down there to see them. The flickers of green and blue light are caused by electrons from Sun hitting Magnetic Field above the poles.

■ Autonomic Nervous System

I work behind the scenes, and you probably don't notice, but it's me that controls your innards. Most of the time I'm in "rest and digest" mode, keeping everything calm. When you get a fright, I'll switch to "fight or flight" mode and will divert Energy to Muscle and the senses. You will definitely be noticing me now!

▽ Autotroph

Eat your greens. Without us autotrophs you animals would not be able to survive. My name means "self feeder," and I don't need to eat anything. Instead I make my own food. Mostly I'll do it using Photosynthesis to trap sunlight's energy for making sugar. However, I can also use stranger chemical processes to get the energy I need.

▷ Avogadro's Number

You can count on me: I'm a constant. My special number tells you exactly how many particles you will find in a specific quantity of any gas. This number is 6,022 followed by 20 zeros. It's a very big number; if you had that many cans of soda, they would cover the planet in a blanket 19 mi. (30 km) thick!

■ Axis

Wheeee! Around you go. I'll stay right where I am, thank you. I'm an imaginary line around which rotating objects spin. Take Earth, for example (or any other planet in solar system). I run right through its center from the North Pole to the South Pole. I stay pretty still—even at the poles where I meet the surface—and the rest of the planet is on the move. When I'm put in my place next to Sun, I'm not a straight-up guy. Instead I'm always on a tilt. This nonchalant lean is what creates Season. Summer is when I lean in to Sun, while winter happens when I tilt away. Just remember, though, I spin you right round, baby, right round.

■ Axon

I'm a nerve cell's main signal cable. I can be as long as an arm (but normally millions of times shorter) and connect all of Nervous System's cells together—every last one. I carry signals as electric pulses through the system. Each pulse is created by a wave of ions flooding in and out of me.

A

B

▷ Bacterium

My motto is "Simplicity equals success." Since the dawn of life, I've done very well by not being bothered with complexity. I am a tiny sack of chemicals and you will find me (and others like me) everywhere—literally. Some of my kind hang out in rocks buried 2 mi. (3 km) underground, or chill out in nuclear waste tanks. Others live in boiling mud, and some can even survive being released into outer space! Not all of us are so hardy, though, and a splash of Water with a dash of bleach poses a danger to many.

We may be invisible, but the world needs us. Bacteria can recycle waste, make soil fertile, and pump out precious Oxygen. Snaking Intestines carries about 2 lb. (1kg) of us, and one trillion of us are grazing on your skin—more than there are people on Earth.

■ Ballistics

What goes up must come down, I say. I'm the branch of Physics that tracks the path of balls, missiles, rocks, and whatever else gets thrown into the sky. I map the constant tussle between forces such as Gravity and Air Resistance to figure out how high, how far, and how fast.

■ Barium Swallow

I'm a drink you don't forget. I'm made of a heavy metal compound called barium sulfate. That is insoluble and totally indigestible and is neither tasty nor nutritious. You glug down this gloop for other reasons. I'm ideal for observing Alimentary Canal, a softy that doesn't show up in normal X-rays. I fill in the gaps so Stomach and Intestines appear clearly on medical scans.

■ Barometer

Feeling the pressure? I can tell you how much. I'm a device for measuring Air Pressure and come in handy when forecasting Weather.

▷ Baryon

I'm a mix of the exotic and the thoroughly normal. I'm a kind of subatomic particle, made up of Quark tripled. Proton and Neutron are both versions of me, but physicists have found

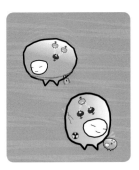

stranger types in nuclear explosions. These have names like "double charmed Xi" and "bottom Lambda." Fancy!

▷ Basalt

Often found under Ocean, I have crystals that are almost too small to see because I'm made from lava that cooled too quickly for them to grow. Under fearsome Pressure, I bubble to

the surface with other minerals. I am famous for making the Giant's Causeway in Ireland: six-sided columns formed from a lava lake that cooled and cracked up like dried mud.

■ Base

"Base" is the chemical way of saying that solutions containing me have a pH above 7. My most common type is Alkali.

▷ Base Metal

I'm solid and dependable, but I don't turn heads. I'm not precious like Gold and Silver. Instead I'm easy to come by and have many uses. They won't make me a celebrity, perhaps, but you know who I am. Iron, Lead, Tin, and Copper—they are all forms of me. In the old days, wacky wizards called alchemists tried to magic me into precious metals—and get super-rich, super-quick.

■ Benzene

A form of Hydrocarbon, I'm a toxic liquid, so stand well back! If you could take a closer look, you'd see that I'm made of six of Carbon's atoms and six of Hydrogen's, all arranged in a ring. The atoms share their electrons, making a buzzing band of Charge around Molecule.

▷ Beryllium

Shy and secretive, I don't get out much. I'm often dug out of the ground as silicates—compounds I form with Silicon and other elements—the most beautiful of which is emerald.

As a metal, I am soft and silvery and used for making Alloy. I make an excellent electrical conductor and am very flexible, too. Because I am so super-light, I also get used in the manufacture of airplanes.

B

▷ Big Bang

I am the start of time itself. I am the beginning of everything. Chapter one. Page one. At first, there was nothing. And then, in fractions of a second, I created Matter, Energy, and order. Scientists can only speculate how, but 13.8 billion years ago I exploded into life in a burst of Energy that has been expanding in all directions ever since.

■ Biochemistry

I'm quiet, clean, and studious, and I'm only just now discovering how powerful I am. You should keep an eye on me. I merge the skills of Chemistry with Biology's power to figure out how Life emerged from a massed march of chemical reactions. Once biochemists figure out how I work inside Cell, they can scale me up to factory size and revolutionize the way things are manufactured.

▷ Biodiversity

Me? I like to mix everything up and get my power from always being different. I'm what makes nature so beautiful, so resilient, and so important. Diversity means difference, and my bio is about adding up all the different kinds of life. There are more than one million Species listed so far, and there could be ten times as many left to find.

▽ Biofuel

I'm the green garbage guy. Old-fashioned Fossil Fuel is made from the remnants of living things pressed and juiced underground over millions of years. I say, why wait? I use organic matter, called Biomass, available right here, right now.

Rotting garbage, crop cuttings, and human waste all release methane. Instead of letting this landfill gas add to the greenhouse problem, I collect it as biogas. Other crops—sugar cane and corn—are grown especially to make a version of me that buses and cars can run on. Sure, producing and then burning me releases Carbon Dioxide, but unlike Fossil Fuel, I'm not releasing CO_2 that's been locked up by Eon. Plus, planting new vegetation sucks it back up. Vroom, vroom, let's burn green stuff!

B

■ Biology

There's more to me than skeletons and specimen jars—alive and kicking, I'm crawling around in the bushes outside! I am the study of Life, taking in animals, plants, and the stranger creatures of the world. I know all about their inner workings and how minuscule Cell, Protein, and DNA help them function.

■ Biomass

I include all living things and everything that comes from them: trees, crops, bacterial sludge, animal waste—and yours! I add up to a lot and can even be used as a fuel.

▷ Biome

We Biomes are earthy characters who have divided up the planet. We are a way to classify similar types of ecosystems around the world. For example, Desert covers Arizona as well as the Sahara. Tropical Forest rings the middle of the world. Our locations depend mostly on Climate and Latitude, so we give the map of the world a striped look.

▷ Bird

All birds have the same template: two legs, two wings, waterproof feathers, and warm Blood. While most of us soar effortlessly through Air, some cannot fly at all!

▽ Bit

I am a very simple type, so simple that I am always either a 1 or a 0. That's it! But join lots of me together in computer-code chains, and I hold all the information in the world.

My pals and I are part of a system called binary, in which each binary digit (bit, geddit?) is a tiny piece of information. Computer's simplest codes—say those that are used to represent the symbols on a keyboard—use just eight bits. And one eight-bit group is called a byte. Four-bit codes are called nibbles because they are half a byte, but bytes normally come in much larger numbers. One thousand bytes is a kilobyte, one million is a megabyte, and one billion is a gigabyte. We bits and bytes can go on and on. The World Wide Web contains 500 exabytes—that's a million trillion bytes!

B

25

▷ Black Body

I am a master of the dark arts. I absorb and emit Electromagnetic Radiation. Astronomers use this idea to find Star's temperature from its color.

▽ Black Hole

Born out of the wreckage of a dying superstar, I am silent and deadly. My black heart forms when the core of a massive star collapses. With such powerful gravity, I destroy "ordinary" Matter as I shrink to a tiny point. Black holes are black because even Light cannot escape from our deadly grasp. We warp Space-Time around us.

▷ Bladder

I'm a pretty simple organ with one amazing talent. I stretch as I fill up with pee, and once I'm around half full of Urine, you start to feel that familiar urge.

■ Blood

Meet the Red Baron, the king of supply and demand! I run a collection and delivery service for the body, and whaddya know, it's a one-fluid operation. The only time you see me is when you cut yourself. Many people are afraid of the sight of me, but there's nothing to be scared of.

I'm a transport coordinator with handy helpers on board. Red Blood Cell carries Oxygen around your body (making me scarlet with pride!). Immune System's white blood cells help battle against intruders. Tiny platelets are little smart guys that clot on contact with Air to form hard, scabby barriers for plugging holes in Skin. Besides Oxygen, I cart nutrients, such as Fat, Protein, Carbohydrate, and essential minerals all the way around your body, mostly sloshing around in my liquid part, Plasma!

■ Bohr, Niels (1885–1962)

This great Dane was the grand master of quantum physics and thought up the best way to understand how Atom works. He showed us how electrons swarm around Nucleus in layers, and jump up and down in "quantum leaps" to take in and give out Light and other electromagnetic radiation.

B

▷ Boiling Point

I'm a fiery cauldron fizzing with rage. Rolling and bubbling, I vent my fury on Liquid. The molecules that make up Liquid are much less tightly bound to each other than the molecules in Solid, but they still have a definite tendency to bunch together. I teach them to stand on their own two feet, by busting apart their intermolecular forces and turning Liquid into Gas!

■ Bond

The name's Bond, chemical Bond. I'm the link that holds atoms together. Without me, Universe would be a cold, thin soup of free-floating atoms, ions, and molecules. I lock on in different ways, making use of Atom's neediness for a stable set of electrons.

■ Bone

I'm pretty hard, but I also have a flexible side—I'll bend before I break. I'm your bodyguard, your knight in shining armor. As Skull, I protect Brain, and, as ribs, I help shelter Heart and your lungs inside a cage. I'm made of stern stuff, I am—from the body's longest bone, in your thigh (femur), to its smallest bone, in your ear (stapes).

I make up the complex framework on which you hang your vital organs. You use me like a set of levers to heave about your limbs. Make no bones about it—without me, you'd be nothing more than a crumpled heap of flesh. You'd think I was dead, but I am very much alive, I assure you. My bone cells are called osteoblasts—they do my maintenance. They work hard to help you grow bigger, and they patch me up when I break. I can last 1,000 years without rotting.

B

▷ Boron

Boron by name but not boring by nature. I'm dull to look at, but that hides a particular set of skills, which I use to make Glass and Ceramic and some dope electronics.

▷ Boson

I'm a particle but not as you know it. I don't make up Matter but carry different kinds of Force. Photon enacts Electromagnetism, while Gluon glues Nucleus together.

▷ Botany

I'm Biology's green side, sticking up for the veggies that flood Air with Oxygen for the rest of you to breathe. My studies take in all kinds of plants—trees, flowers, ferns, and moss. I can look inside Plant Cell to see Photosynthesis at work, and pull back to understand why Biome contains different plants, depending on where it is.

■ Brackish

Well, I am not sweet or sour, but I'm not really salty either. I'm halfway between Ocean's acrid salt water and the fresh water of River. Living in me is a specialized business.

▷ Brain

Peabrain or egghead, I make you the person you are. I am the boss of your thoughts, memories, dreams, hopes, desires, and your mysterious sense of yourself. Wrinkled like a walnut, I'm not much to look at, but I rule!

My "head office" is divided into departments. The brain stem is your life-support system. It controls automatic functions, such as breathing and Digestion. The cerebellum is a mini-brain in charge of balance and movement. At my core, an egg-shaped thalamus processes information from my numbskull nervous pals, while the hypothalamus is important in responses to cold, hunger, and pain. My outer layer—the cerebral cortex—deals with all those clever functions that include reading, writing, and speaking. Heady stuff, indeed!

■ Bronze Age

I'm all over now, but I used to be the state of the art. Around 5,300 years ago, people figured out how to mix Copper with Tin to make tough bronze objects. The rest is history.

▷ Brown Dwarf

OK, so I'm no dazzler, but characters like me are the missing link between Star and Planet. The runt of the star-birth Nebula litter, I simply lack enough size to kick-start nuclear fusion in my core. Shy and retiring, I glow weakly, but don't take me lightly. I'm 13 to 80 times heavier than Jupiter.

B

▷ Brownian Motion

Everything about me is random! Seen under Microscope, tiny Pollen will jitter around in Water as if it's alive—well, that's what Mr. Brown the botanist first thought. Mr. Einstein the physicist said the grain is being battered by the motion of molecules in the liquid. This insight led to proof of Atom's existence and explains how Diffusion works.

■ Buckminsterfullerene

Named after a designer, I'm Carbon's biggest allotrope, a hollow ball made from 60 carbon atoms arranged in hexagons and pentagons.

▷ Bunsen Burner

The undisputed king of the lab rats, I burn like a beacon, taking center stage in a theater of bangs, bubblings, and strange smells. I'm used for flame tests (to identify what type of Metal is in Compound) and for heating stuff.

Invented by Mr. Bunsen, I have an air hole at my base, near a gas inlet. With the hole fully open, the air-gas mixture has a high Oxygen content, allowing complete combustion to create a roaring-hot flame. But watch out! On this setting, my flame burns an almost invisible blue, with two very distinct cones—the hottest part is the inner cone. When you just need me on standby, switch to my cool, orange-yellow safety flame. Closing the hole allows Gas to mix with Air only at the head of my chimney, which results in incomplete combustion and a safer, cooler flame!

■ Buoyancy

Sink, swim, or float? I'm here to figure that out. Objects in a fluid—Liquid and Gas—are pushed on by the fluid around them. If that force is weaker than the weight, an object sinks. If the object is very lightweight, the "buoyant force" pushes it upward. If the two forces balance, then it simply floats where it is. It was Archimedes who figured out this system while wallowing in his bath. The idea came to him in a flash of inspiration. "Eureka!" he shouted, which is Greek for "I have it!"

■ Burette

Are you good at concentrating? It's my job to measure Solution's concentration—that is, how much stuff is dissolved in it. I'm a slow-working tube and tap. Drip by drip I mix colored indicator chemicals to run my tests.

B

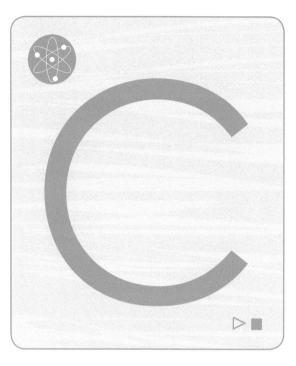

C

■ Calorie

I'm quite an old-timer as an old-fashioned way of measuring Energy. Today I have a new lease on life telling you how much Energy is in your food. I am measured in a very flashy way. The food is burned super fast and creates Heat, which is then used to warm up Water. Every degree warmer for every gram of water equals one of me!

▷ Capacitor

Need Charge? That critter is on me somewhere. I'm an electricity store used by Circuit to add a boost on demand. I'm lying underneath a touch screen. Feel?

▷ Calcium

They call me "The Scaffolder" because I make up a large portion of the bony types that hold you together—Skeleton and Tooth. I'm needed in large amounts as you grow, helping build the tough calcium phosphate that makes up Bone. As you get older, I keep your frame strong.

In my pure state, I'm a reactive metal with a soft, silvery appearance. However, I'm also a bit of a hard man. When my ions dissolve in Water, it becomes "hard"—detergents won't lather, soap forms a surface scum, and limescale forms in your coffee maker. I've been known for centuries and am found in common compounds, such as lime, cement, chalk, and Limestone. All of these are white, have been used in construction, and also have the ability to neutralize acid.

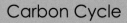

▷ Capillary

Tiny and oh-so-fragile, I thread my way through your body to feed it with life-giving, oxygen-bearing Blood. I'm all over you like a rash, from the tips of your fiddlin' fingers to the tops of your twitchin' toes. It's through yours truly that Blood reaches Skin, so you can blame me for all your gushin' blushes.

▪ Carbohydrate

Yum, yum, food chemicals like me are such sweeties, you'll know us for sure. I'm sugar and all things nice, but also tasty, toasty Starch, found in cereal and bread.

▷ Carbon

A master of the black arts, I'm a stealthy element that can morph into many forms – black charcoal, hard and brilliant diamonds, slippery graphite, wonder material graphene and buckminsterfullerene balls. My ability to form several types of chemical bond with myself means I can whip into all sorts of shapes. With so many different guises, there's a whole branch of "organic" chemistry devoted to me.

I form the bulk of all living matter. Almost everything you eat is a carbon-based compound – fats, sugars, fibre, you name it. I move about the planet and Food Web in an endless cycle that sees me released from food in breath and body waste, absorbed by plants and eaten again. Carbon Cyle will tell you all about it.

▷ Carbon Cycle

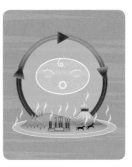

An important global process, I put Carbon on an endless spin cycle to keep Life, well, alive. My complex, five-part program involves living things, Earth, Air, Ocean, and human activity.

The cycle starts when animals breathe out Carbon Dioxide and plants take it in from Air, using it to build themselves. Animals then eat the plants and breathe Carbon Dioxide back into Air. When plants and animals die, carbon stored in their bodies gets locked into Earth as sediment. Meanwhile, a lively and constant exchange of gases goes on between Atmosphere and Ocean.

C

31

▷ Carbon Dioxide

I'm CO_2, the colorless, odorless Gas used to give sodas their fizz. Plants use huge amounts of me during Photosynthesis, while animals are busy breathing me out.

▽ Carbon Footprint

I add up the CO_2 a person, object, company, or country emits. I read the emissions as footprints, and they mostly come from burning Fossil Fuel. Your footprint might come from buying clothes made in faraway places, heating Water for a bath, or watching TV! If you want to cut down, walk to school instead of going by car, and buy local food.

▷ Carboxylic Acid

I may be an acid, but I'm a mild-mannered type. I'm found in natural products, such as coconut oil (lauric acid), milk (lactic acid), and vinegar (acetic acid). As salicylic acid, I provide pain relief in the form of aspirin. If I have more than ten of Carbon's atoms, I'm called a fatty acid, many of which are essential in the body.

■ Carnivore

Smile, please. Show me your teeth? Do you want to see mine? Long and sharp, aren't they? That is because I'm a meat eater—that is what my name means in Latin. You'll find my kind in all animal groups. There are even plants that snap up or snag a meaty treat. Meat is full of nutrients, but it is hard to get hold of. As a result, there are far fewer of me than there are of Herbivore, my plant-eating pal.

▷ Cartilage

The knee bone's connected to the thigh bone, the thigh bone's connected to the hip bone . . . connected by me! Soft and pliable, I'm your flexible friend. You'd be as stiff as a board if Skeleton was made from Bone alone, and I stop it grinding against itself at joints (ouch). I also make the soft stuff, like Ear and the tip of Nose.

C

▽ Catalyst

Chemical engineers love me because I smooth the way for Chemical Reaction, allowing it to proceed more easily. Despite all the hot stuff going on, I keep my cool and don't get used up in the course of the chemical craziness. I help produce most industrially important chemicals—you name it, I catalyze it! My jobs include refining petroleum, breaking down Hydrocarbon's chains, and producing ammonia in the Haber process.

I often allow intermediate compounds to form, providing a new pathway for a reaction to follow with lower activation energy. With less of Energy being used to start a reaction, it can happen at lower temperatures—and faster, too. I can also work by providing a larger surface area upon which a reaction can take place.

■ Caterpillar

Goo, goo, gah, gah. I'm a baby butterfly—and I'm hungry. I know. I know. I look more like Worm, and I don't have wings. But look closely, I've got six little clawlike legs, plus some fleshy stumps that help me walk. I'm not built to flutter like Mom and Dad because I'm a larva, a type of Insect infant that does just one thing: eat. I will eat many times my own weight. (I like Leaf, mostly.) Eventually, I'm full, and I slow right down to a dead stop. I might look dead, but I've grown a thick skin called a chrysalis. Protected inside, my wormlike body is transforming into an adult body. I am what I am, and I'm going to be a butterfly one day.

■ Cathode

Don't touch me, I'm an electricity contact and the results could be negative. Actually, I'm always negative. When you next fit a battery into a gadget, look for the minus sign—that's me. When switched on, I'm Circuit's negatively charged part. My neighbor Anode is always more positive than I am. Keep me away from him.

■ Cathode Ray

I used to be a magical mystery, then I was welcomed into every home, and now I'm very uncommon. I'm an invisible beam that flows out of Cathode when it is electrified in Vacuum. In 1899 I was used to discover Electron—you see, that's what I am, a stream of electrons. A few decades later, my rays were lighting up faces across the world, because the first TVs worked using a cathode-ray tube. My beam made hundreds of bright dots on the screen—get the picture?

C

■ Cation

Ion by name and positive by nature, I'm what metal atoms become as they lose electrons. You'll find me at the Cathode.

■ Caustic

I give a nasty burn, so you had better watch out. I describe Acid and other chemicals, such as bleach cleaners, which attack whatever they come into contact with. My powers are perfect for cleaning away unwanted gunk and germs, but I'm dangerous, too—so always take care around me and stay safe.

■ CD

My name is short for compact disk. A layer of Aluminum sandwiched between plastic, I started a revolution by converting Sound's waves into Digital's code. Read by Laser, my code becomes music to your ears. DVD (digital versatile disc) does the same with movies and games. Let's party!

▷ Celestial Sphere

Understanding the stars is difficult, and I'm here to help. Those twinklers are scattered through space, but from down on your planet, they all look the same— small and bright. Astronomers invented me to make a map of the lights on the inside of a giant sphere, with Earth in the middle. I'm not real, but take a look up at me; I offer a cosmic show.

▽ Cell

All great things come in small packages, and I'm no exception. I am the definitive building block. Everything that happens in your body happens because of me. I might be small, but I'm no lightweight, I can assure you!

Put me under Microscope and you'll see what I mean. Inside cool plasma Membrane, I'm busy working with all sorts of chemicals to make everything you need to keep your body functioning. Dig a little deeper and you'll find Cell Nucleus. This limited-access area is my control center and home to genius gene-giving DNA.

I don't like to work alone, though. It takes millions of me to make up your whole body. I divide to make copies of myself, so there are always enough of me to go around.

C

▷ Cell Nucleus

Welcome to Cell's headquarters. If you need information, then you are in the right place. I'm a double-bagged data center right in the middle of Cell. Inside me, I store DNA in Chromosome's vaults. I keep that data safe and only send it out for reading as RNA. Don't worry, you'll get the message.

▷ Cell Phone

Choose me when you want to make calls or send texts on the go, and I'll use Radio Wave to zap them through space. I use batteries to power me up when I'm feeling low.

■ Celsius

Is it hot in here, or is it just me? I'm all about checking on Temperature using a system devised by Anders Celsius in 1742. He set my zero point at the freezing point of Water, and my 100 at the point when Water boils.

■ Center of Gravity

I'm the point in any object where Gravity acts. For something rounded and regular, like Earth, I'm right in the middle, but for more complicated shapes, I'm not so simply located. An easy way to find me is to stand an object up and let go. Gravity will pull on me, and if I'm off-center things just fall over.

■ Centrifuge

My name means "flee from the middle," and my high-speed spin pushes things out with great force. I help train pilots and astronauts learning to work in fast-moving craft.

▽ Ceramic

Ancient in origin, I am smooth, glassy, and cold. I am hard enough to stop a bullet, resistant to chemical attack, and impervious to Heat. I refuse to be bent and am way too hard to be cut. I may sound tough, but I am brittle and shatter easily. Because of this, I tend to be cast as a single piece. Early ceramic materials were clay, but today's advanced ceramics use crystals of silicon carbide, zinc oxide, zirconia, and silicon nitride. Highly durable, they have many uses, from car disk brakes to bulletproof vests.

C

■ Chain Reaction

Once I start, I just can't stop. I'm a kind of reaction where the products feed into the reactants (the raw ingredients of a reaction). So once a reaction starts, it just gets faster and faster. Chain reactions are seen in Chemistry. The ozone hole in Atmosphere was made by one. A nuclear chain reaction is used inside bombs.

■ Charge

I'm the property of Matter that forms the basis of Electromagnetism, and when I get moving, I make Electricity. There are two sides to me. Electron has a negative charge, and Proton has a positive one. My opposites attract, but when I'm alike I'm completely repulsed.

▷ Charon

I'm often in the shadow of my dwarf planet pal, Pluto. I'm described as Pluto's moon, but I'm one-third of its size, so we are really a double Dwarf Planet system. I'm an ice world in my own right. I'm named after the boatman who ferried the dead to the ancient Greek underworld—the realm of Pluto.

■ Chemical Formula

I show how Element combines to make Compound. My system links the elements' symbols and the number of the atoms. My most famous form is H_2O, the formula for Water. "H_2" means two Hydrogen atoms and "O" equals one Oxygen.

▽ Chemical Reaction

I'm gunning to get a reaction. I'm what chemistry is all about. When compounds bump into each other, chemical bonds get broken and Atom, Ion, and Molecule make new alliances. You can tell if I'm around— Compound changes color, Thermometer goes bonkers, and Precipitate appears out of nowhere. In short, my process is a chemical change where one substance is transformed into another.

I combine ingredients like a master baker. Sometimes there is no going back to the substances you started with—like baking a cake. I either suck up Energy in an endothermic reaction or I give Energy out in an exothermic reaction. Chemists can zip around from one product to another, to synthesize the one they need.

C

■ Chemical Symbol

Element is a simple fellow, but he comes in many forms, such as Hydrogen, Gold, and Iron. Many of the elements have different names in different languages, and that can make chemists get very confused. To keep everyone on message, the world's chemists have agreed to give each element a symbol made up of one or two letters.

■ Chemisorption

I'm a complicated process where Liquid or Gas is absorbed onto a surface and held in place by a chemical bond. Catalyst does it a lot, and it is also happening during Corrosion when Water clings to Iron.

▷ Chemistry

Chemistry is one of the top three sciences, along with Physics and Biology. Chemists study the stuff the world is made from— Matter's physical and chemical properties— and how it behaves when Chemical Reaction gets involved. This is the field that has given humankind a hundred thousand snazzy new materials, not to mention an understanding of the inner workings of Life itself.

■ Chemosynthesis

Welcome to the dark side. I'm a process similar to Photosynthesis, but instead of energy from sunlight, I will use Chemical Reaction to power food production. I'm found only in Bacterium and Archaea.

■ Chemotroph

With a name that means "chemical eater," I am a microbe with a difference. One kind of me eats Rock's chemicals. That's right, I literally eat stone. Other kinds eat no food at all, nor do they get Energy from sunlight using Photosynthesis. Instead they use chemicals harvested from hot springs to make sugar. We're weird, but scientists think we might be one of the oldest forms of life on Earth.

▽ Chlorine

One of the Halogen gang, I'm a toxic gas whose choking fumes can kill. I'm mostly put to work battling Bacterium in swimming pools and toilets. It is me that keeps you safe from waterborne diseases such as cholera and typhoid. Adding small amounts of me to drinking water has saved millions of lives.

C

▷ Chlorophyll

I might be the single most important chemical on the planet. I drink in Energy from Sun and use it to power the production of sugar—food for plants and, ultimately, for all  things on Earth, too. As if this wasn't enough, the process also produces Oxygen—the gas all animals breathe—and sucks up that nasty greenhouse gas Carbon Dioxide. (Photosynthesis will tell you all about that.) I put the "green" in greenery. Because I absorb blue and red light, but not green—which is reflected back—I give plants their color. In the fall, many plants get rid of me, and their leaves turn a golden yellow.

C

■ Chlorophyte

Small and always green (the clue is in my name), I am a type of Alga. It's the "chloro" part of my moniker that hints at my color, because I am packed with Chlorophyll. That's the clever chemical that helps me and others like me store food as Starch. Like Alga, I can be single-celled or multicelled, and most of the time you'll find me living in Fresh Water. Not always, though—there are members of my group who prefer Seawater, while others spend their time clinging to trees and rocks on land.

■ Chloroplast

I'm the place where Photosynthesis actually does its work. I'm a tiny green blob rammed full of Chlorophyll. Mostly I'm packed inside Leaf's cells.

▽ Chromatography

Anyone in need of a little TLC? Slide over here—I'm your main squeeze! Although chemists might need some tender loving care every now and then, they're more likely to be happier with thin-layer chromatography (also TLC)! I love a good joke, but I'm also a full-fledged lab rat, with serious uses. With my exciting crime-stopping streak, I bring some color to the lab!

I'm used to separate Solution's mixtures. Try me out for yourself. Just make a dot with a marker close to the bottom of a strip of filter paper, dip the end into a shallow dish of water, and leave it overnight. As Water seeps into the paper, the components in the ink mixture separate themselves out at different rates. This is how CSI teams analyze dye found at a crime scene.

■ Chromosome

Call me picky, but I like to keep things tidy. That's my job inside Cell Nucleus. All that DNA would get everywhere (and break apart) if I were not there to keep it in order. The long DNA molecule is coiled up inside me, wrapped around a frame of proteins. Human cells have 46 of me, but that number varies from species to species.

▷ Cilia

We are little hairlike structures around the edge of Cell. We waft together to make a current in the water around us and are used to collect chemicals from the surroundings.

All together we have a much larger surface area, which makes that job much easier.

▷ Circuit

I bring together the items needed for Electricity to flow and be useful. I make a one-way round trip for Current to take and create Work along the way.

■ Circulatory System

Guess what, I'm a system that circulates stuff. I'm a network of pipes that moves Blood and lymph around the body, and I ensure that every inch of it is fed and watered—and swept clean, too.

■ Classification See Taxonomy

▽ Climate

People tend to get me confused with Weather, but I'm nothing like that changeable dude. I'm solid and dependable. You see, Climate is what you expect, Weather is what you get. Day-to-day weather is unpredictable, but over the years a pattern starts to emerge, and that's where I come in. I am the typical weather that a region has through the year. Places close to Earth's equator get a stronger blast of Sun's energy, so tend to be hot. They may also be very dry (Sahara desert), or very wet (Amazon rainforest). I like to change slowly, but over the past 100 years my changes have started speeding up. This will have effects for the whole planet and its people.

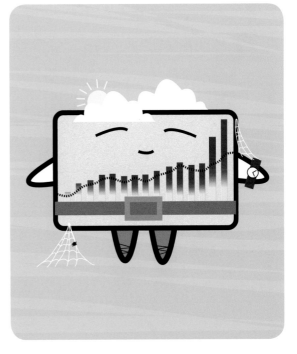

C

39

▽ Climate Change

Check me out—I'm a total hottie! Sure, I might sound cozy, but I spell trouble for the planet. Some say I'm a fairy tale—they wish! I'm real, all right. I am right here, right now, and I'm going to bring major change.

No one knows exactly what will happen as Earth heats up, but one thing is for certain: a big thaw. Frozen water—say, Glacier—melting will cause flooding so that islands and low-lying areas will find themselves below the waves rather than above them. Ecosystems will change in polar regions and newly flooded zones. With less ice, less of Sun's energy will be reflected back into space, resulting in more warming, and even more melting. Can humans stop this from happening? I can't tell you, but it sure is something to think about.

C

▷ Clone

My siblings and I are a collective of 100 percent identical organisms, all created artificially. The genomes of our offspring are exactly the same as those of our parent. Let's clone! Take an egg cell, suck out its DNA, and inject into it Cell Nucleus within the animal you want to clone. Modified Cell can grow into a new body—a body that is identical to the one it came from.

■ Colloid

I'm a mixture in which material is evenly spread out in Liquid or Gas, just as it is in Solution. However, the particles of material are too big to disappear like they do when they dissolve. So I become a cloudy swirl. Fog, milk, and ice cream are all forms of me.

▷ Combustion

I am a type of Chemical Reaction that occurs when fuel combines with Oxygen in Air. That gives off Heat and has Energy to burn. I'm a warming influence on a cold day, but I can also burn everything to the ground. My burning generates oxidized products, which can become Pollution. They include toxic carbon monoxide, and Carbon Dioxide, a gas that is charged with Climate Change.

▷ Comet

I'm like a dirty snowball hurtling through space. When I get near Sun, I give off a long glowing tail. You might know of Halley's Comet, which is due back in 2061.

▽ Compound

My creations are the perfect pudding—a combination of all the right elements in just the right proportions. Chemicals like to cozy up with each other, and with the help of Ionic and Covalent Bond, I allow them to do this in a way that benefits both elements. But once my ingredients have been fused together, it's difficult to separate them.

■ Computer

The ultimate user-friendly utensil, I can be anything you want me to be: video player, number cruncher, game machine, musical instrument . . . anything. All I need is an input—some Bits and bytes for Microchip to process—and I'll make an output.

It's a team effort, really. At my center is a processor that runs a program. I also have a memory chip that holds on to important data while I work. I just love to hoard stuff and save files on a hard disk for later use. My user (that's you) inputs commands using a keyboard or mouse—or even his or her voice—and my output can be monitored on a display, or screen. Sure, I can work alone, but I really shine when I'm jacked into the Internet. That way I share data and deeds with billions of my kind. Wow!

▷ Concrete

I may not be beautiful, but I am certainly cheap, and that has made me the planet's most popular building material. Together with Steel, I have built the world. Bridges, roads, skyscrapers, pipes, and dams. All me! To make me, you add cement, gravel, and sand to Water to make a sloppy mixture that can be shaped with molds and left to set as hard as Rock.

■ Condense

I'm a bit drippy. That's kind of what I do. I'm the process where Gas turns into Liquid as it cools down—like boiling in reverse.

C

■ Conductor

Move along, please, I'm a carrier of Heat or Electricity. I'm usually Metal, and I'm the opposite of that blocker Insulator.

▷ Conifer

I am the tallest and longest-living type of plant. For many I am the symbol of Christmas, and "spruce" up the season. I keep my needle-shaped leaves all year. Even a blizzard won't get me down—my sloped sides form chutes so heavy snow falls away. I invented Seed about 370 million years ago and store that critter inside my cones.

▷ Conservation

My mission in life is to save, not money but nature. Like a green superhero, I want to preserve the animals, plants, and wild places of the world. And I need your help!

▷ Constellation

I'm the pattern that ancient astronomers saw in the stars. I once showed animals and heroes in the heavens, but now I refer to sky regions, like the countries on a map.

■ Consumer

Excuse me, I hope you don't mind if I continue eating. That is really what I am all about. I am a living thing that eats, or consumes, other living things.

▽ Continent

I am one of the Magnificent Seven—North America, South America, Antarctica, Africa, Europe, Asia, and Oceania. We are the thick parts of Earth's crust that poke out above Ocean. We are full of goodies that you dig up and use to keep yourself fed, to manufacture things, and to power your machines. We've been around for four billion years, trundling here and there around the surface, supported by Tectonic Plate, bumping, rippling, and fragmenting, very, very, very slowly.

C

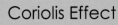

■ Copernicus, Nicolaus (1473–1543)

Copernicus made the world go around—around Sun, that is. Before him everyone believed the Sun went around Earth.

▷ Copper

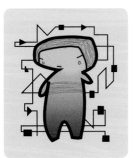

I am an age-old Metal that gave birth to whole chunks of history and launched civilizations. Mixed with Tin to make bronze, I have been used for centuries to create ornaments and practical tools. I am unique among metals in that I have a red hue. Some of my compounds are vivid blue or green. I am an exceptional conductor of Electricity and Heat, so I'm used in wiring and pots. You'll find me in Microchip, too.

▷ Coral

I live in a high-rise colony. Our white, calcium carbonate apartments might be a squeeze, but there's always plenty of clear, unpolluted water, good light, and warmth. What's known as a "coral head" is actually a vast colony of colorful, genetically identical polyps, each only a tiny fraction of an inch across.

Many hands make light work, and there is no shortage of labor here. Most of us build slowly and steadily, but we are master masons. For proof, just look at the Great Barrier Reef—it is visible from space! We operate a strict one-polyp, one-house policy, with nutrients piped in via a system of canals. We've also teamed up with Alga, who takes energy from Sun and provides us with food.

▷ Core

Right at the heart of things, you'll find me inside Atom, Planet, and Sun. Inside Earth, I'm mostly Iron, together with a bit of Nickel, and I take credit for making Earth a giant magnet. It's hot, enough down here to melt Metal. My outer layer is Liquid, but my hot heart is squashed back into spinning Solid.

■ Coriolis Effect

I'm a spooky effect that makes Rocket and aircraft appear to swerve in flight. However, they are going straight, and it is Earth beneath them that is moving out of the way!

C

■ Corrosion

Give me a chance and I will turn you to dust. My destructive chemical power attacks Metal with Water and Salt to make flaky characters like rust and other chemicals that slowly weaken whatever you make. You can ward me off with paint, oils, and other clever coatings.

▽ Cosmic Microwave Background

I'm the biggest beamer in history. About 13.5 billion years ago, Universe cooled down enough in the wake of Big Bang for Atom to form. That released a vast blast of Energy, creating a flash so bright that we can still see it in the sky. My blinding flash now involves invisible Microwave that shines out from the whole sky. Telescope maps me to learn about Universe's structure.

■ Cosmic Ray

I am Universe's speed freak—a tiny object, such as Neutron or Alpha Particle, that is whizzing through space almost as fast as Speed of Light. When cosmic rays hit Atmosphere, they collide with atoms to produce exotic subatomic particles, and electrify Air. It's cosmic!

■ Cosmology

I am the study of everything—where it came from and where it will go. I am the science of how Universe came to exist. I'm an offshoot of astronomy, and my team of scientists is investigating things like Gravity, Dark Energy, and Cosmic Microwave Background to find out how Big Bang came about.

■ Covalent Bond

I'm a cuddler, a bit of a clinger. What I have, I give to you (as long as you promise to share with me, too), and in this way I'll hold most types of Compound together. I'm a bond that forms between two atoms when they share their outer electrons so that they each fill their neighbor's electron shell. That makes Atom calm down and stay stable. I normally form between two nonmetal elements.

▷ Crude Oil

Call me petroleum, or even Black Gold. I'm the dark oozer from deep underground that contains many useful chemicals such as gasoline and paraffin wax.

C

▽ Crust

Beauty is skin deep, but that's fine with me—I've got all the looks! While Core and Mantle may be hot stuff, I'm the face of Earth and the one with all the scenery. Some may point out that I'm just solidified scum that floated to the surface when Earth was young and molten, but we all know that yummy cream rises to the top.

I'm thicker in some parts than others. Just like a reflection in crystal-clear Lake, the shapes I form at the surface are mirrored below. So, beneath Mountain's range, huge "antiranges" poke down into Mantle. Basalt lies under most of Ocean, and granite forms Continent. On top of this there is a thin scraping of Sedimentary Rock, made mostly from ground-up pieces of Igneous Rock and dead organisms.

▷ Crustacean

I'm a class of creature with jointed legs—often ten or more—pincer mouthparts and a skin toughened with shell to make some armor. I breathe using gills. Mostly you'll find my kind in Water as a crab, lobster, or shrimp. My main ambassador on land is the pill bug or wood louse.

▷ Crystal

I'll make you a Solid—always the same one, over and over again. I'm the main way of creating solid substances. You see, inside me, Atom is arranged in a rigid structure that is repeated millions of times over. The repeats build up to make shimmering sparklers, flaky powders, and even Metal.

■ Curie, Marie (1867–1934)

Marie Curie did more to unlock Radioactivity's secrets than anyone else. She discovered new elements and even invented a mobile X-ray truck for scanning soldiers during World War I.

■ Current

I go with the flow—in fact, I *am* the flow. I can be a movement of Air or Water, but mostly I'm known as the motion of electric Charge to make Electricity.

C

Darwin, Charles (1809–1882)

Charles Darwin was famous for monkeying around with our ideas about Biology. He made the most startling of suggestions—that Species (things like humans, pigeons, and daffodils) can change with time. This is a dog-eat-dog world; it's also a beetle-eat-dung and a lion-eat-man world, and only the fittest survive. Those that are best at surviving when the environment changes live to fight another day. Natural Selection will tell you more and will explain how it completely changed the way we view the world.

Day

I set the pace as Earth's preset clock. I start at midnight and keep on going for 24 hours, until it's time to start all over again. I'm kept ticking over by Earth's spin.

D

Dark Energy

A type of antigravity, I am a silent force driving Universe apart. In truth, I am a bit of a mystery. Even though astronomers can see my effects, I appear to come from nothing.

▷ Dark Matter

Cloaked from detection, I'm pretty much invisible. I don't interact with any form of light radiation, so I can't be seen on any of the frequencies used by astronomers to explore Universe—whether it's Radio Wave, Microwave, Infrared, visible Light, Ultraviolet, X-Ray, or Gamma Ray. Although I shy away from the limelight, I use Gravity to pull on "ordinary" Matter, and it's this pull that gives me away. I explain many weird things, including the speeds of stars inside galaxies and Light warping around invisible objects!

Deceleration

Slow down, you're going way too fast, it's time to make use of me. You see, I'm Acceleration, but going the opposite way. When it comes to me, instead of making stuff go faster, Force works against Motion to slow a thing down.

Decibel

Speak up! Can't hear. What? Nope, can't hear. Either you are too quiet or I am too loud. It's actually my job to indicate which. I'm the measure of loudness—call me dB, for short. A normal conversation is roughly 60 dB, and a whisper is down at 30—I said 30—dB. An emergency siren is 120 and, listen carefully to this part, if I get up to 140 (a firework close to your ear can do that) then I will start to damage Ear for good.

Deciduous

Drop it, I'm the process that puts the leaf fall into autumn. When Weather is cold, it damages flimsy Leaf. Green Chlorophyll is broken down, leaving just red-brown chemicals beneath. Then that old withered Leaf gets released and flutters down to the ground. Don't worry! Trees grow fresh leaves in spring.

Decomposer

I hate fresh food. I want it to be long dead, rotten, and perhaps covered in dung. I take the form of Bacterium or Fungus, and I clear up the remains of dead Organism.

Deforestation

I fell Forest to make way for farmland or an urban zone. At the time people might think I'm a good thing to do, but I destroy so much Life that will never regrow.

Delta

I clog up River's mouth with a mess of mud and tiny channels. I form soft, squishy land. I'm a hodgepodge, but it's not really my fault. I'm built from the sludge that big, brown, muddy River carries down to Ocean. I am born when River flows too lethargically to carry its silty load out to sea and the sea is too slack to wash it away.

D

■ Dementia

I forget, but I know I'm a common disease among older people. Gradually they lose their memories as I shrink Brain.

▷ Density

I'm the measure of how compact materials are. The more Mass in anything, the denser it is. Dense things cram a lot of mass into a small space, which makes them feel heavy in your hand. Sink or swim, it's all because of me. Less dense things will always rise above denser things. This is why balloons filled with lighter-than-air Helium sail skyward.

▷ Desert

Stay far away if you value your life. I am a dangerous Biome with a lethal track record. That's because you're wet, soppy things, and I am dryness personified. My regions include the world's most arid places. Some of them have seen barely a drop of Precipitation for years. Feeling thirsty yet?

I can be served either hot or cold. Hot deserts are mostly found fairly close to Equator. Cold ones, such as Asia's Gobi desert, are closer to the poles. Although I'm a place humans dread, amazingly I'm not barren of Life. Some plants and animals have adapted to my harsh conditions extremely well. Reptile is often quite at home in hot deserts. Its ability to go for long periods without food and to survive on very little Water means I suit it very well.

■ Diffraction

Along with Reflecting and Refracting, I am a wave behavior, and, just watch, I'm spreading. When Wave—sound or light, they are all the same to me—meets a narrow gap, most of it cannot fit through. The part that muscles past the gap then spreads out in all directions, filling in what was there before. This is the main reason why Sound travels around corners.

■ Diffusion

I get everywhere, because I am a common property of Matter—the one that makes it spread out so it is evenly spaced. All my particles do not work together. They are just ping-ponging around at random, bashing into each other. However, Motion always ensures that crowds of stuff thin out.

D

■ Digestion

I make things simple: eat food with its complicated chemicals and Enzyme will help break it down into raw materials for your body to use.

▷ Digital

While Analog grafts information onto Wave, I turn it into code—a string of zeros and ones, to be precise. My code is used in phones, TVs, radios, and Computer.

▷ Digital Camera

I store images as digital files and can display them instantly on an LCD screen—no fussy negatives here! My pictures can be edited, cropped, and retouched with ease.

▷ Dinosaur

The world has seen nothing quite like me. From terrifying T. rex to massive Argentinosaurus, I am an ancient type of beast that thrived for 160 million years—the largest land animal ever to have lived. My name means "terrible lizard." Even though my pals and I are all long gone, scientists called paleontologists continue to find our bones in million-year-old Rock. These remains give clues to an animal's lifestyle: teeth that shred Leaf look very different from those that bite chunks of flesh or crack open seashells.

■ Diode

It's my way or nothing, that's all I'm saying. I'm a component in Circuit that allows Electricity to pass in only one direction, and never the other way. I rely on Anode and Cathode to keep things moving. When switched on, Electricity runs from positive Anode to negative Cathode.

■ Direct Current

I'm built from a surge of electric charge that just keeps on coming, always moving in the same direction. I put the DC into "doing cool stuff" because I'm the kind of electricity made by batteries. That's right, it's me powering up all your electrical devices— flashlights, cell phones, and remote controls included. Diode converts jittery Alternating Current into smooth me.

D

Disaccharide

I'm a kind of sweet stuff made from two sugar molecules locked together. The most common is sucrose, which is made from glucose paired with fructose. Sucrose is the sprinkling sugar used in baking and also squared up into lumps. One lump or two? Other versions of me are Lactose (seen in milk) and maltose.

Dissolve

I make things disappear—as if by magic. I'm a type of mixing where a solid, liquid, or gas substance (a solute) spreads out among the molecules of Water, or some other Solvent. When I happen, Solid, Liquid, and Gas simply slip from view. They are still there, but you cannot see them anymore. Once dissolved, Mixture becomes Solution.

Distance

I'm all about space, a measure of how far it is between one place and the next. I'm fundamental to all measurement.

▷ Distillation

I'm a bootlegger and old-school scoundrel. My technique purifies and separates two or more liquids. Every Liquid has a slightly different Boiling Point, so heating up a mixture of liquids brings each one to a boil at a different temperature. In this way, I drive off the substance with the lowest Boiling Point first and collect it in a separate vessel.

▽ DNA

Some think that I'm a totally twisted individual, but while my slinky curves turn heads, I'm quite a bookish character. I'm so astounding that within my graceful folds and sinuous switchbacks lies the secret of Life itself. Cell has a library made of me, called its genome, stored for safekeeping inside Cell Nucleus. The human library has 46 "books" in it, called chromosomes.

The pages are filled with coded instructions, called genes, that are technically blueprints for making you . . . you! From the color of your eyes to your height. Most of the words in the books are gibberish, however, and scientists have yet to understand the purpose of this "non-coding" DNA. Although 99.9 percent identical to all other humans, that tiny 0.1 percent is enough to make you unique.

▷ Dome

Like Arch, I have a rounded structure that directs heavy Weight sideways instead of down. It means I have no need for indoor walls or pillars.

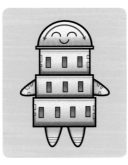

◼ Dopamine

One of several crucial chemicals called neurotransmitters, I slip across Synapse to carry messages from one nerve cell to the next. The message I bring is one of calm and contentment.

◼ Doppler Effect

I'm a spooky phenomenon that works with Motion to change Wavelength. You'll hear me during an emergency when a vehicle siren's pitch swings lower as it speeds past. Sound is squeezed into a high pitch as it approaches you, and then stretched into a deeper tone as it moves away. I do the same to Light's waves, causing red- and blueshift, an important feature of starlight.

▷ Drought

I am the ying to Flood's yang. A sustained period of fine Weather, I might sound promising, but don't be fooled. I bring terrible dry spells that parch the land. Life without Water is impossible. Vital crops and livestock perish, and starvation looms for all. Once I'm in place, I'm hard to shift: I drive away all the moisture from the ground. Soil turns to dust, and I start making Desert. Thirsty yet?

◼ Ductile

Heave! I'm the ability to be pulled into a wire. Gold and Copper are highly ductile.

▷ Dwarf Planet

Have you seen me and my pals? No? Okay, we are small and hard to find. Unlike the full-scale planets, we share our orbits with Asteroid and Comet, so we are hard to spot

among the crowds. We are still big enough to be globe-shaped though. Astronomers have found five of us so far, including Pluto and Eris, but some say there could be hundreds of us out there.

D

E

▷ Earth

With the perfect conditions for surface water, I'm the only known planet that can protect and nurture Life. One big ball of Metal and Rock, I have a liquid-metal core at my center. Core generates Magnetic Field, which protects me from Sun's radiation.

More than two-thirds of me is covered in Liquid—Water, to be precise. Next comes Atmosphere, that thin layer where Weather likes to hangs out. The thin shell covering my surface is called the biosphere. That's where you will find the likes of Ocean and Biome, both teeming with Flora and Fauna.

■ $E = mc^2$

I'm the most famous equation in science (according to me, that is). I'm all about Energy (E) and Mass (m), and I show that each is the same as the other. How much Energy is there in something, you ask? You just multiply Mass by Speed of Light (c) squared. Light moves very quickly, so you will end up with a huge number as your answer.

▷ Ear

Listen up, I'm totally wired for Sound. My shell-like parts channel vibrations in Air into your ear hole. These rap on my skin-tight eardrum, which passes the beat to three tiny bones: the malleus, incus, and stapes. These tap a signal on the cochlea, a fluid-filled, shell-shaped tube. Each ripple in the fluid twitches nerve endings that connect with Brain.

▷ Earthquake

I shake things up. Everything trembles before my mighty power—Mountain, Ocean, Forest, even skyscrapers and highways.

I can be destructive, but I can't help it. Earth's plates don't move smoothly, but squeeze past and push up against each other, causing Pressure to build. Suddenly something gives, and I am let loose with a release of Energy. My shock waves cause the ground to quake. Powerful quakes heave Tectonic Plate all over the place. Quakes on Ocean's floor can set off giant waves called tsunamis, which travel at great speeds and can cause destruction.

▷ Echinoderm

Excuse me, darling, VIP coming through! I am the star of the sea—at least, my starfish type is. Its many arms drip with jewel-like spines, and it brings color to the drab rock and sand of the seabed. A starfish is pretty special. It can change color and will grow a new arm if an annoying snapper fish breaks one off.

They say beauty is skin deep. Well, my skin is toughened with plates of bone—my name means "spine skin" in an ancient language—Greek, I think. Other members of my family include the unruly spiked sea urchins that prick a swimmer's feet. Like the starfish, they have a mouth on their bottom and a bottom on the top. My family also includes sea cucumbers (quite bland, like the vegetable), sand dollars, and sea biscuits.

■ Echolocation

I let animals use Ear to see—almost. In the dark there is no Light to illuminate the surroundings, so animals give out short, sharp Sound (mostly high-pitched), which echoes off whatever is out there in the dark. The echoes help an animal build a picture of what is around it. That picture is updated with each echo, updated with each echo . . .

■ Eclipse

I cast shadows that block out Sun and our Moon. In a solar eclipse, the Moon passes between Earth and Sun, blocking out all its light. The world goes dark for a few minutes in the middle of the day. A lunar eclipse is when Earth stops sunlight lighting the Moon. The Moon's disk is turned red by Light as it passes through Earth's atmosphere.

E

■ Ecology

I'm the science of connections and relationships in the living world. Any description of the ways in which plants and animals live together involves working with Food Web and Habitat, mixing in Climate, and perhaps taking a look at Biome. I show that living things rely on each other for survival as they fight to get enough food and other resources to survive.

■ Ecosystem

Ecologists often talk about me, but I'm something of an enigma. I'm a community of wildlife that live together in a particular way. Understanding my relationships helps Conservation protect rare Species. However, look for me in the wild and I'll blend into a complex web of life that covers Earth.

E

■ Ectothermic

I'm the system where an animal's body matches the temperature around it—you might know me better as "cold-blooded."

▷ Egg

Graceful and gorgeous, I ripen in Female's ovary once a month. I float dreamily down the Fallopian tube, hoping that speedy Sperm is on his way to see me. I'm an easy target—85,000 times larger than Sperm in terms of volume. Each of us has a half-set of chromosomes, and if Sperm makes it in time, these fuse to create a brand-new being. Then, deep within the protection of the uterus, I start to grow into a baby. But there is a catch! We only have 24 hours, and if Sperm doesn't show, I exit during a period so that another egg can try in four weeks.

▷ Einstein, Albert (1879–1955)

With his crazy hair and even crazier ideas, Einstein turned Physics—and all of science—on its head. He did that by linking Energy with Mass with his famous equation, $E = mc^2$. Einstein also had ideas about how space and time are related. Pretty good for someone who rarely went to school!

■ Ejecta

While Lava goes with the flow, I am shot up into the air by Volcano during an explosive eruption—ash, stones, even giant rocks. And what goes up must come down. Take cover!

▷ El Niño

As a tricky character, always up for a laugh, I mess around with Current in the Pacific Ocean and affect Weather all over the globe. I might be a kid at heart, but after Season, I have the largest short-term impact on Climate. Even now, Climate Change gets blamed for the havoc I wreak. Oh, I do love getting away with stuff like that.

By switching the direction of Current in the Pacific Ocean (close to Peru), I make Weather drier than normal in the east and wetter in the west. Atmosphere spreads these changes worldwide and affects Weather in local places. I've been playing hide-and-seek for ages, but that game is almost up. Meteorologists are beginning to understand my global effects. I might not be the wild card for much longer.

E

▷ Electric Current

No question, I'm the hero of the past 200 years. Without me, there would be no TV or phones, and Computer couldn't work! Pretty dull, eh!

As a sparky form of Energy, I can be turned into Light, Sound, or Motion, but I need a complete circuit to work. The chemical Potential Energy in a battery provides the "push" to move Electron around. I zap around Circuit in the blink of an eye, but Electron actually moves very slowly. Be careful—my jolts jangle up Atom, Cell, and nerves in your body, giving you a nasty shock. Too much of me is lethal.

▷ Electric Generator

All your energy needs are met by me. Quiet and unassuming, I do my work behind the scenes, but with dash and panache, if I may say so.

My flair is for "magicking" Electricity out of thin air using Electromagnetism. It's simplicity itself. Spin a coil of wire inside Magnetic Field, and Electron gets up on its toes and moves—you have found yourself Electric Current. The secret of my success is that fundamental Electromagnetic Force is made up of magnetic and electric fields. If only one field is there, Electromagnetism has the knack of automatically generating the other.

▷ Electric Motor

I am a sparking wizard! Before your very eyes I change invisible Electricity into Motion. I may seem commonplace—I open windows in cars, drill holes in walls, and spin discs in DVD players—but think again! I rely on the incredible phenomenon that a wire carrying Electric Current generates Magnetic Field around itself. Make a loop of this wire and you have Electromagnet. Stick that next to a second magnet and each will spin toward the other. I reverse my current's direction every half-turn, so the magnetic poles flip, and that makes the loop spin like crazy. Voilà, you have instant power!

▷ Electricity

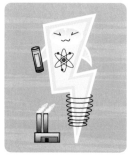

A common source of energy for machines, I'm a lively type—sometimes high voltage—so be careful when I'm around. I am made up of Atom's negatively charged electrons. They dash around, trying to rush toward positive protons. Whenever there is a difference in charges, I step in to even things out.

My electrons whiz through Circuit to make Electric Current—a simple metal wire is all I need. I can be stored inside a battery or fired out by a power plant whenever needed.

■ Electrode

I have contact. I'm the place where Circuit connects to Power. Anode and Cathode will tell you all about it.

■ Electromagnet

You can turn me on—and off again. I come about when Magnet gets its pulling power from Electricity. At the flick of a switch, Magnetic Field disappears. I come in handy in so many ways, not least in Electric Motor and in automatic locks and switches.

■ Electromagnetic Radiation

I'm a set of waves that are released when Electron gives away Atom's energy. Some waves are visible—that's Light—but the rest are not. The gang also includes Radio Wave, Microwave, Infrared, Ultraviolet, X-Ray, and Gamma Ray. We use Speed of Light to travel as fluctuations of electric and magnetic fields. The difference is in the energy we carry. Radio is weakest, and Gamma Ray is the most powerful.

E

▽ Electromagnetism

Forget those two circus clowns, the Weak and Strong Forces! No doubt they've been filling your head with their hot air about how powerful they are. Welcome to the real world! Gravity and I are the only forces that matter outside the ridiculously tiny distances of the atomic nucleus. You actually *feel* us.

In an electric field, I cause attraction between opposite-charged particles and repulsion between like-charged particles. I also keep Electron happy hanging around Atom, get Electric Current moving, and allow Matter to hold its shape. I stop you from sinking through your chair and prevent your hand from going through this book as you read it. I'm the dream-team combo of electric and magnetic fields, and I get around using Speed of Light.

▷ Electron

I'm a negative particle that zips around the outer regions of Atom. With a negative charge equal to Proton's positive charge, I am constantly drawn toward it. I make all your electrical gadgets work, from TVs to smart watches and electron microscopes.

■ Electron Shell

I'm a many-layered concept. Electron cannot just go anywhere when it joins Atom. Instead it takes a place in me—a layer or shell. Each one of me holds a set number of electrons, and that is what gives Atom its unique structure. Once the smallest, inner shell is full, a larger one further out from Nucleus starts to fill up.

■ Electronegativity

I'm the measure of Atom's pull on bonding pairs of electrons during a chemical reaction.

▷ Electroreception

Super senses do not get zappier than me. I'm the ability to detect the tiny pulses of Electricity being made by Nervous System and in Muscle. I'm used by a shark's snout and a platypus's duck bill to help find tasty prey in the deep dark water or lurking hidden in mud.

E

▷ Element

Pure and simple, I am the basic stuff of everything that you see in Universe. With my 118 unique versions and almost no limit to the possible combinations, there's already a mind-boggling number of compounds in existence. Chemists continue to make new ones by combining me in different proportions or in new ways.

Made from atoms, each of my varieties is determined by the number of protons that Atom's nucleus has. My lightest variety is Hydrogen, with a single proton in its nucleus. Next up is Helium, with two protons and two neutrons. This pattern continues all the way to the strange, unstable, and very short-lived elements with one hundred or more protons (and attendant cargo of neutrons) in their central nuclei.

E

▷ Embryo

I'm a new being, but in the very early stages. In human terms I form two weeks after Sperm meets Egg. After growing for six weeks, I become a fetus.

■ Emulsion

Often oily, I'm a gloopy mixture of two liquids that do not get on. Give me a shake and I'll become a cloudy brew of minute droplets. Let me stand and my constituents will try to separate into distinct layers. Paint, salad dressing, and milk are all kinds of me. Adding a surfactant keeps the droplets together and keeps me from separating.

■ Endemic

It's not where you're from, it's where you're at that's important. Maybe so, but to help understand Ecology, biologists need to know where animals and plants originate, and that is where I come in. I mean that Species is in its original home. My opposite is exotic—that happens when Organism is introduced to a new region.

■ Endoplasmic Reticulum (ER)

My name has a complicated sound to it, and rightly so. It means "internal membrane network." I'm made up of tubes and chambers that surround Cell Nucleus. My job is to make chemicals and transport them. I become rough ER when I'm studded with ribosomes. It is inside me that Ribosome reads Gene.

■ Endothelium

You've got me under your skin. Well, perhaps that is not quite right. I'm like Skin, but instead of being on the outside of the body, I line the internal surfaces of the circulatory system, such as inside Vein and Artery.

▷ Endothermic

Give me your energy—I need it. Do not fight me, it will be mine. I'm the opposite of Exothermic, and I'm the name for when Chemical Reaction takes in Energy from the surroundings.

I may need an energy boost to get going, but in the end I make everything colder.

▷ Energy

Call me boastful, but I am everything. I am everywhere—even inside you—and I have been around for ever. I'm pretty spooky stuff, too, because you can never see me, you can only see what I *do*.

Don't listen to anyone else—I'm the dude that gets stuff done around here. Sure, Force and Motion get together to make me do the work, but without me they'd be nothing. How else would the stars twinkle or atoms smash together? Who else could bring the groceries home or make the TV work? These things only happen because I'm there. Every machine needs a source of energy to convert into a more useful form. I might go in as motion energy, but I come out as Heat, Electricity, Light, or Sound—all of them kinds of me. But not for long . . . I feel a change coming on.

■ Enthalpy

A complicated way of simply saying "heat" or the energy inside a substance.

▷ Entropy

I am the king of chaos who makes sure that Energy always changes from useful forms to messed-up, spread-out forms. A renowned troublemaker, I'm the reason why things break and burn out, and I'll get you, too, in the end. I work in one direction only, making more chaos. A room always gets messier, never tidier by itself. To clean up, you need to put some effort in. But I'll always be back.

E

▽ Enzyme

I'm a catalyst, which means that I speed up your body's chemical reactions without getting used up or altered in the process. You'll find different types of me all over your body. I make chemical reactions happen faster, while saving on Energy. Who is it that cuts your food into simple molecules for your body to use? Yep, that's me! And who helps make all those proteins that keep you alive? Right again! And because I am unaffected by the reactions I cause, I can repeat the job thousands of times a second.

E

■ Eon

Some call me Aeon, and my meaning has gotten confused over the years. Everyone agrees I'm a very, very, long time. Most round me up to a period of exactly one billion years.

■ Epidermis

I've got you covered. I'm the biological term for the outermost layer of any complex life form. That could be Skin or the surface of Leaf. Both are different, sure, but both are also me, and as such they do the same job. I keep Water in the body—and stop extra Water from getting in—and I prevent germs and other bad guys from getting inside, too.

▷ Epigenetics

A mysterious spirit beyond nature and nurture, I am a chemical overlay that determines whether Gene is expressed. I can make any cell type in your body—muscle, nerve, skin—just by expressing or switching off, and by boosting or muting individual genes. I explain why one identical twin might have asthma when the other doesn't. Pure Gene-ius!

■ Epiphyte

Plants sometimes feel the need to put down roots in their own patch of earth. Not me. I actually grow on other plants and let them do all the hard work. Sometimes I take Water from Air, or I might drill into my host and steal its water (and sugar). I might grow on myself—and then I become an epi-epiphyte.

■ Epithelium

I'm like Epidermis, only not as tough. I don't need to be because I cover the internal surface of animals, making up the gums and lining of Lung and Intestines.

▷ Equation

Sometimes you have an answer but don't know the question. At these times, my letters stand in for the numbers that you don't know. Say Tyson is 4 years old and Rosie is 26. At

what age will Rosie be three times Tyson's age? Well, in x years from now, Tyson will be 4 + x and Rosie will be 26 + x. Written as an equation, she will be three times older than he is when 3(4 + x) = 26 + x. You can eliminate the numbers that you do know by writing the same equation like this: 26 − (3 × 4) = 2x. So now you know that 14 = 2x, which means that x = 7. When Tyson is 11, Rosie will be 33. It's as easy as *a*, *b*, *c*—or *x*, *y*, *z*!

▷ Equator

As the longest and most important line of Latitude in the whole wide world, it would be easy for me to become big-headed. But it's not in my nature. I am an even splitter who girdles Planet like a big belt. When it comes to taking sides between north and south, I don't just sit on the fence—I *am* the fence! Slap bang on the world's hottest, steamiest parts, I am roasty toasty.

I might be just a line, but I am a significant divider. In some places, my path is painted on the ground so that people can have the pleasure of putting a foot in both hemispheres at the same time. At sea, sailors sometimes have a ceremony when they first cross me. I have even given my name to two countries: Ecuador, which I run through, and Equatorial Guinea, which is not far from me.

■ Equid

Why the long face, you say? Well, I'm the scientific name for horse-like creatures, and not enough people have heard of me. As well as horses, I include donkeys, wild asses, and zebras. So now you know—pass it on.

▷ Equilibrium

In perfect balance, I am a place of complete calm and stillness in a Universe that is otherwise full of chaos. Every Force pulling, pushing, or twisting me cancels its opposite out, so I'm not going anywhere. But if one of those factors changes, then I'll lose it, for sure.

E

■ Eris

Twice as far from Sun as Pluto, when I was first discovered, I created havoc in the world of astronomy. Icy, distant, and mysterious, I'm the largest of the newish group of Dwarf Planets. Before getting my official name from the Greek goddess of discord and strife, I was known as 2003 UB313. I have a partner in crime—a companion moon named Dysnomia, after the Greek god of lawlessness!

▷ Erosion

Think you're hard? It doesn't matter how tough you are—I will wear you down. I'm the name for when Force grinds Mountain to dust. Big-bruiser Rock trembles at the

thought of me. Water and Wind do most of my heavy work. Ocean's waves ceaselessly pound on coastlines, while River and Glacier sculpt land by rubbing against it.

■ Erythrocyte: see **Red Blood Cell**

■ Escape Velocity

How fast do you have to go to get out of this place? I can tell you. I'm the speed needed to break free of Gravity's pull. For Earth, that is 7 mi. (11 km) per second. For the Moon, where Gravity is weaker, it is only 1.5 mi. (2.3 km) per second. Black Hole's gravity is so enormous that its escape velocity is faster than Speed of Light—so nothing ever really escapes.

▽ Ester

I'm a fruity fancy! Wreathed in the fragrant fug of a flowery bouquet, my molecules can be all the flavors and colors of a scented eraser collection: strawberry, cherry, lavender . . . you name it. When fresh, I give natural fruits and berries their taste and smell; when fake, I am the main ingredient for artificial food flavorings.

I get made in the pretty sounding esterification reaction, when Acid reacts with Alcohol. (To make the peary smell in pear candy, for example, pentanol is added to ethanoic acid.) You can whiff me in Air because I am more volatile than Acid and prone to Evaporation. At full strength, I am found in all kinds of industrial solvents, such as insect poisons. I am so much more than just a fake flavor!

▷ Estuary

A curious mix, I'm half River, half Ocean. Wherever River reaches the end of its journey, Fresh Water mingles with the salty sea. River's flow will have slowed by this time, and Tide

takes over, moving water upriver and then downriver. In me, Water often becomes Brackish. It has a saltiness that changes as River takes on more water when Ocean surges in and out twice a day.

■ Ethanol

Hiccup! I'm the alcohol in beer, wine, and other alcoholic drinks. I'm made in nature from sugars. All alcohols are poisonous, but my toxic effects are weak, and they are what makes drinkers drunk.

■ Evaporation

I'm the name for the process in which Liquid turns into Gas when exposed to Heat. This usually happens just below Boiling Point.

■ Event Horizon

Beware all who enter here—don't cross me. I never forgive, and I will instantly forget you. I'm Black Hole's outer rim, and the point at which nothing can escape Black Hole's mighty pull of Gravity. Anything that travels across my line is sure never to make the return journey, not even Light. For that reason no one will ever, ever know what happens beyond my boundary. It remains an eternal mystery.

▷ Evergreen

Little Leaf stays on me all year round. Sure, I drop old ones, but I also grow new ones at the same time. Evergreen trees grow in Rainforest and other habitats that are green for the whole

year. We also grow in cold places, where there is not time to grow leaves in the spring.

▽ Evolution

In the ancient past, life on Earth was not the same as it is now. That shows us that living things change, all thanks to me. I work using a process called Natural Selection—check the dude out to learn more.

E

▷ Excretion

No time wasters here. I lay waste to what the body does not want. I handle the leftovers from meals that the body has rejected— I'll dump that for you. I also work with Kidney to sift out the garbage from Blood. The result is Urine, a liquid gold that keeps the body clean. I'll do whatever it takes, even adding waste to sweat and tears.

▷ Exoplanet

I'm really out there, a planet orbiting another star far from Sun. I was first spotted in 1995, and since 2009, Kepler, a space-based smartie, has been picking me out among the stars, one by one. Kepler's finding so many of us that astronomers now figure we're more common than stars! Most of us seen so far are big, like Jupiter, while the little rocky exoplanets are tough to track. Kepler has spotted 30 top picks to be checked for Earth-like features. You never know, if one looks habitable, it could be home to aliens.

■ Exothermic

Really, I'm a complicated way of saying "gives off heat." An exothermic Chemical Reaction releases Heat—often as fire! A big hitter in my team is Combustion, which releases useful amounts of Heat from Fossil Fuel. The heat is on!

■ Experiment

How do all the others know anything? They could be just making it all up. Well, I'm here to make sure that does not happen. I'm a test system used by scientists to check out Theory. To do that they must predict my results. If they get them right, then Theory rings true—and can be used in this book!

▽ Explosive

Living life on the edge, I have a nasty habit of going off with a BANG! My destructive power comes from Energy stored in my chemical bonds. Many of us are based on elements that join together very tightly— Nitrogen, Carbon, and Oxygen. When their bonds break, they release Energy very quickly, in a rush of expanding Gas and Heat. It's a blast!

E

■ Extinct

Gone, but not forgotten. I spell doom for every species of plant and animal. At some point, one type of critter's time will be up; the last member will die, and I will have prevailed. Oh, so you think humans will avoid me. Let's wait and see. Almost all Species that have appeared on Earth are now extinct—only about 1 percent are alive today. Evolution ensures new Species appear as fast as old ones die out, although every so often the system crashes and a big chunk of Life dies in a catastrophe called mass extinction.

■ Extracellular

I'm on the outside, beyond Membrane. I refer to anything outside Cell. Often I'm a Liquid that bathes Cell.

■ Extraterrestrial Life

Out of this world! I don't exist—at least no one's found me yet. You might know me better as an alien. Scientists called astrobiologists are looking for me.

▷ Extremophile

Turn Heat up—I like it hot, hot, hot! There's nothing I like better than to take a dip in a boiling hot spring. I also live deep under Ocean, loitering around Hydrothermal Vent—the scalding "black smoker" that pumps out Heat and Mineral. Far from Sun's rays, I take my food and Energy from the vent itself—this may be how life on Earth began.

▽ Eye

Clap your eyes on me! I'm an eye-poppin' marvel that just has to be seen. I am a true visionary who brings your world into glorious all-color focus. You can certainly rely on me to see the bigger picture!

I work a little like a camera, but there's more to me than point and shoot. Thanks to six dedicated muscles, I swivel about to look around (all the better to goggle you with!). My black center, your pupil, is actually a hole, and your pretty, colored iris a muscle that I use to control the amount of Light that comes in. A lens behind your iris focuses Light on my back wall—your retina—and, presto, there's an upside-down image (well, nobody's perfect). Thankfully, Brain flips the image the right way up so you won't think that you're standing on your head!

E

Fahrenheit

I'm the old-school cool who decides what's hot and what's not. Celsius has taken over most of the world, but I'm still Temperature's leading scale in the United States. I have some quirks, such as the freezing point of Water being 32° of me, and body temperature set at 98.6°. I'm named after Dutchman Daniel Fahrenheit, who set me up in 1724.

Fat

Whenever you need me, I'll be right there, a store of Energy packed away for the bad times. Just be careful you don't hoard too much of me. In animals, I'm often thick and waxy because my molecules are easily tangled. However, I can also be a greasy slime ball who oozes as an oil, and this is how I generally appear in plants.

▷ Fault

A real splitter, I am always cracking Rock up. Continent is riddled with deep, underground cracks like me, and I'm running through Ocean's floor, too. Whenever I break

open or shift my rocky flanks, I cause quite a shock, and it can end up as Earthquake. I do destroy, sure, but I also create. The Atlantic Ocean is getting wider thanks to me, and I'm slowly reshaping dry land. All my fault!

Fauna

A word used by scientists and other smart folks, all I really mean is "animals"—basically the animals that live in a certain place or time period. I'm almost always knocking around with Flora. Go check her out.

▷ Feldspar

We form two mineral families: the K-feldspars and the plagioclase feldspars. Between us, we are the world's most abundant minerals and make up almost

two-thirds of Earth's crust. We have been found in Meteorite and all the way across Solar System. We crystallize out of liquid Magma and form a major part of Rock —metamorphic, igneous, sedimentary— you name it. We are found in ornamental buildings and many household cleaners.

▷ Female

One of the two sexes in nature, I get together with Male to make offspring. In some cases I can even do it alone—that's what makes me different from Male. It's my job to make Egg and give her everything she needs to do the rest of the child-making business.

Femur

Lanky with long shanks, I'm the lengthiest bone in the human body. I run from your knee to your hips.

Fertilization

I am the creator, a producer of new Life. I was involved in making you, and you, and you. When Sperm combines with Egg, I'm there to merge them both into a brand-new individual —similar to others, but always unique.

▷ Fertilizer

Spread over fields, I put back into the earth the elements that growing plants take out. Without me, the land wouldn't support decent crops for long. But don't mess with me. Used too much, I make soil too acidic to grow plants and cause algal blooms in waterways. Those guys use up all of Oxygen and stifle Life. You have been warned!

▽ Filter

I'm a canny operator who can get you out of a fix. Got Solid mixed up with Liquid? I make quick work of separating them. With the aid of a filter funnel and a cone of filter paper, I create a barrier that lets Liquid through while blocking chunky Solid. No job is too small. You'll even find me making your mom's coffee—well, filtering out the coffee grounds before she drinks it.

Fire

Definitely too hot to handle, I'm a flamin' good source of heat energy, but also a blazingly bad power of destruction. My flames are made of hot Gas that is reacting and giving out Heat and Light. To extinguish me you must take away one of my three ingredients: Fuel, Oxygen, or Heat.

▷ Fish

When I arrived on the scene 500 million years ago, I caused a splash! My pals and I were the first animals with backbones, and we've been braving the waters ever since.

We range from deep Ocean to River and flooded caves. We are the world's top swim team—most of us have a gas bag called a swim bladder to keep us afloat. We don't have legs, just fins, but a few of us can flip-flop around on land, and some can even fly!

In most of us, Skeleton is made from tiny, sharp bones. Watch out, you don't want Bone getting stuck in your throat. One notorious gang of fierce fish, with sharks among them, uses rubbery Cartilage instead of Bone. Ha! Be careful not to get stuck in *their* throats!

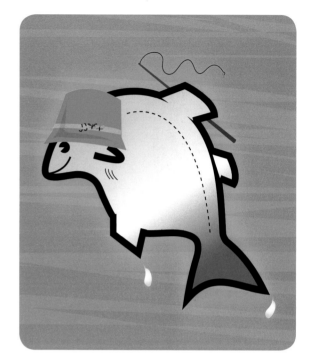

F

▷ Fission

Just one little Neutron can make the big, wobbly nuclei of some elements split in two and release a blast of Energy. This process is used to generate Electricity in power plants, propel nuclear

craft, and make nuclear bombs go boom. With such awesome Power comes great responsibility: I produce waste that remains dangerous for tens of thousands of years.

▣ Flora

I'm a local collection of plant life. I may be petals and perfumes and all things nice, like Flower, but I also include weeds and all.

▷ Flower

I'm a seductive temptress with one thing on my mind —to spread copies of myself. I come clothed in the loveliest of colors, with a fiendish array of love traps, perfumes, and

sweet nectar to lure Insect, Bird, and even bats to help me complete my mission.

I have male parts called stamens, which produce Pollen. My female part, called a pistil is made of a stigma and an ovary. Pollen from another flower tunnels into the pistil to reach an ovule inside my ovary. The two combine to make Seed. My pretty parts then die away, and my leftovers grow into Fruit.

▽ Flowering Plant

Before I came onto the scene, the world must have been a very dull place. Conifer is so stern and stiff, and Seedless Plant is all dressed in drab greens and browns. I am utterly fabulous, though—a real stunner—and bring vibrant color to Earth.

My relatives and I are very image-conscious. Our arrangements of color and perfume attract animals. We want them to pay us a visit so we can get them to carry Pollen to our neighbors. Some of us, such as grass, are content to bend with the wind— that spreads Pollen just as well. We are also important to you humans. A lot of your food comes from us—wheat and rice, corn and oats, most vegetables, peas and beans, oils, fruits, and nuts. We even provide the cotton fibers for your clothes.

■ Fluid

I'm a catch-all term for Liquid and Gas, and I group them together because they can flow —unlike stiff Solid, which is stuck in its place.

▷ Fluorine

Wild and dangerous when pure, once tamed by Chemistry I form lots of useful compounds, such as Teflon, the famous nonstick coating. You'll also find me in toothpaste, protecting Tooth. Be warned, I'm a deadly Gas that burns through Concrete. My power comes from a competitive streak. I will take electrons from almost any atom.

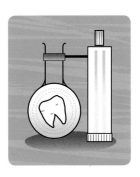

F

■ Food Web

I am the planet's biggest foodie, and I keep tabs on exactly who's filling their stomachs with what—or whom. My networks are impossible to escape—every living thing, including you, is caught up in them. These interconnected paths show how animals and plants in an area interact or, more straightforwardly, who runs from whom.

I get complicated pretty quickly, so another way of looking at me is to say that I show how Energy moves around in any environment. The solid base of every one of my networks—in every Biome, that is— consists of plants. They take in Sun's energy to make their food and ultimately provide Energy and food for the entire living world. Maybe you are what you eat, but I am what everyone eats!

Forces

You think we're pushy? Well, some of us can pull, too. Our job is to transfer Energy from one thing to another, and we get absolutely everywhere. We have four fundamental forms. Electromagnetism pushes Electric Current along wires, while Gravity makes things fall to the ground. Strong Force holds Atom's insides together —it has to pull really, really hard to keep that guy from splitting apart. Weak Force pushes Particle out of Nucleus when Radioactivity makes Atom unstable.

F

Strong Force

Holds an atom's nucleus together.

Inertia

A feature of Mass that resists Force's action.

Weak Force

Creates fission, fusion, and radioactivity.

Electromagnetic Force

Builds everything from atoms and magnets to light and electricity.

Friction

Created as surfaces rub against each other in passing.

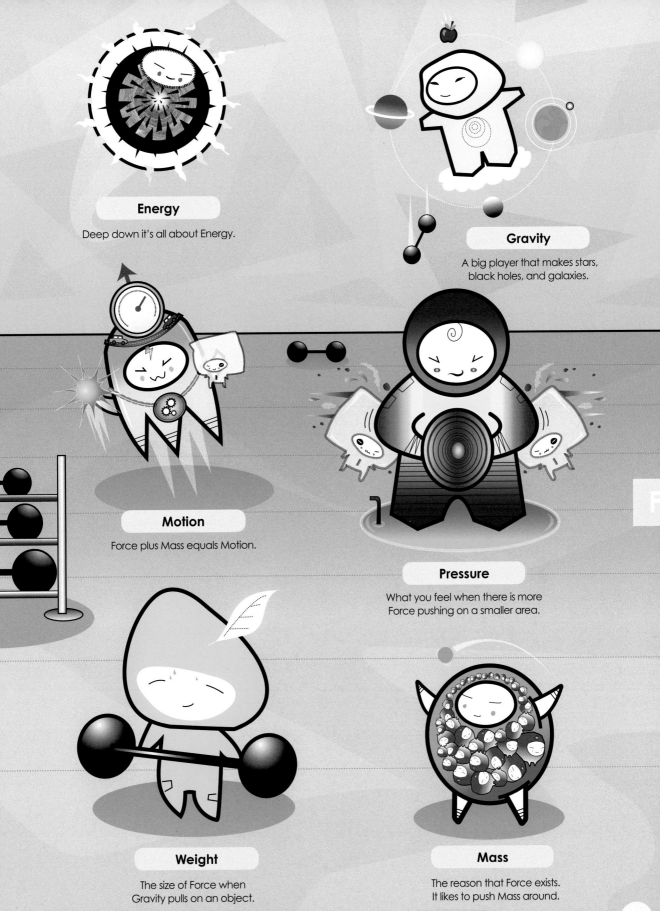

Energy

Deep down it's all about Energy.

Gravity

A big player that makes stars, black holes, and galaxies.

Motion

Force plus Mass equals Motion.

Pressure

What you feel when there is more Force pushing on a smaller area.

Weight

The size of Force when Gravity pulls on an object.

Mass

The reason that Force exists. It likes to push Mass around.

▷ Force

I invite you to feel the force! You can't see me. You can't hold me. But you sure can *feel* me. You can feel me in the grip of your tires on the road; when you kick a ball hard and send it flying; if you've ever struggled to lever open a can of baked beans; or if you've reeled around in a country dance. I overcome Inertia to push, pull, and twist things around, but I have a tendency to get out of control. When moving things crash, I go haywire and create a mangled wreck.

I have one golden rule: for every bit of me that gets produced, another (equal) bit of me is produced in the opposite direction. This simple policy stops your feet from sinking into the ground when you walk. It is also how Rocket travels and why running into a wall is a bad idea!

F

▷ Force Field

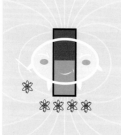

Spooky and invisible, I'm the ghostly area where Force is at work. If you want to get to know me, find a couple of magnets and get a feel for how I surround them.

▪ Forest, Temperate

Climate is totally temperate in my regions. I am generally found in parts of North America, Europe, and northeast Asia. I won't stand for long, cold winters, and every Fall, as Weather cools, my broad-leaved trees perform a magnificent change of color before they drop their foliage in a grandiose display . . . that leaves me naked!

▪ Formula

In mathematics I show the relationship between one value and another. If you know one value, I'll tell you the other.

▷ Fossil

I offer the only way for animals and plants to live on millions of years after they die —by turning them to stone. My secret spell is mineral-rich Water creeping through Rock. As organic parts of a once-alive thing rot, Mineral moves in and takes their place. The process is called permineralization. Trust me, hard as Rock, I'm here to stay.

▽ Fossil Fuel

Some say I'm a dirty fuel because I'm not renewable like Tide and the wind. But you need me to help Electricity power essentials such as heating and cooking. My forms—Coal, Oil, and Gas, come from living things that die and are buried deep inside Earth.

Coal was once plant material from ancient swamps. Oil was squashed from the bodies of tiny sea creatures. Gas is burped up when Coal and Oil are squeezed inside Earth. Energy stored by these prehistoric life forms when they were alive is released when I am burned. In most places I am mined and drilled out from far underground, but sometimes I move naturally up to Earth's surface. Slinky Oil can be refined to make sparkier fuels such as gasoline, diesel, and aviation fuel.

■ Fractional Distillation

My job is to sort out a slippery bunch of oily characters. Take petroleum, a mix of many hundreds of hydrocarbons that are not much use all muddled together. I heat that thick oil so it boils. The gases rise up my fractionating tower and then begin to cool down. The lightest "fraction" of chemicals—things like gasoline—make it all the way to the top before becoming liquid again. Heavier fractions, like wax, paraffin, and kerosene, condense faster and lower down my collection tower. Thanks to my organizational skills, crude petroleum is tidied into fractions all ready to do their jobs.

■ Free Fall

I'm flying without wings—in other words, falling straight down. If the only force acting on me is Gravity, Motion just gets faster and faster. However, if Air Resistance turns up, then my free-falling fun meets with Terminal Velocity, who sets a top speed.

■ Free Radical

I'm like a bull in a china shop, if the bull is high-speed Atom or Molecule whizzing around . . . and the china pieces are chemicals. Basically, I smash stuff up on an atomic level.

▷ Freezing Point

See Melting Point for full details, but I'm the same thing, only in reverse. Instead of warming up so Solid becomes Liquid, I chill things out so Liquid turns into Solid.

F

▷ Frequency

I'm the most important measure of Wave. It's me that counts because I tell you how many cycles—or identical patterns of Wave—pass by. The higher I am, the more peaks and troughs I get through every second. This is measured in hertz, and—before you ask—no, it doesn't "hertz!"

Generally speaking, the greater the frequency, the more energy Wave carries and the greater its penetrating power. This is especially true of Light. High-frequency Photon can burn and damage cells in your body. Ultrasound, above the range of human hearing, can boil an egg, but is also used to make scans of babies in the womb. Infrasound involves low-frequency rumbles, such as whale song, which can travel for many miles through Ocean.

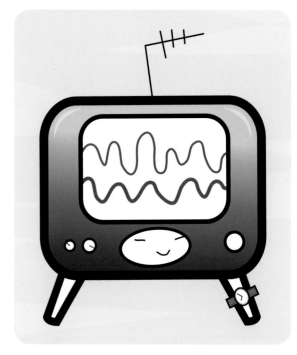

F

▣ Fresh Water

Life-saving, salt-free liquid loveliness, I'm the water in rain, River, Lake, and ice. Only when I reach Ocean do I get salty.

▷ Friction

I'm no smooth operator, that's for sure. No, everything's a drag with me. I'm the force that stops things from sliding around easily. I lurk among all the tiny lumps and bumps that cover surfaces and that get stuck on each other. I'm not all bad, though. Without me, Wheel would just spin endlessly, instead of rolling. It's a rough life, but that's me all over.

▷ Fruit

Don't mix me up with vegetables. See a Seed? Then you've found me. I am often full of natural sugar and make a healthy snack. Eating me helps Seed disperse.

▣ Fuel Cell

I am the green dream. Unlike a short-lived battery, I sup a continuous supply of Hydrogen from a tank and take Oxygen from Air to power electrical systems. My only other output is water vapor. While polluting engines and motors chug away, I run cars cleanly and quietly—a breath of fresh air for a sweeter-smelling future, perhaps.

Fundamental Forces

Universe follows a few rules. One of them is that all Force comes from four prime sources: Gravity, Electromagnetism, Weak Force, and Strong Force.

▷ Fundamental Particle

So, Proton and Neutron are important, for sure, but they are not like me. I belong to the set of 17 smaller particles that make all Matter and Force. Most are quarks and electrons, plus photons and other bosons. Physicists get their best description of Universe by having us work as a team.

▷ Fungus

I know I'm often a bit yucky, but don't forget me—I have a kingdom of my own. Even so, I am the poor relation of plants and animals. You give me unlovely names like dead man's fingers, death cap, and stinkhorn. Of course, that might be because I can be deadly when eaten.

You are most likely to see me in damp Forest, where I send toadstools and mushrooms out into the open. But that's just the tip of the moldy iceberg. Mostly I'm made from a mass of wispy threads that is hidden from view. And I like to spread out, sometimes covering a huge area. I am nature's cleaner. I love dead bodies and any pieces of rotting waste. I slowly devour it all, gradually turning it into sticky mush until there is nothing left.

Fusion

I love high-pressure situations. When I really feel the squeeze, that's my time to shine. I am a nuclear reaction like Fission, but instead of one big Atom splitting in two, I make two small atoms merge into one. That process releases Energy (several times as much as Fission), and it's me that makes Sun shine: two Hydrogen atoms in its core get squished into one Helium. All stars are fusion reactors like this. Engineers are building Earth-bound reactors to tame me as a new source of clean power. However, so far, these projects take in more of Energy than they give out.

Futurology

Want to know how we will live in the future? I use today's science and technology to give a good guess—we'll find out soon enough.

F

G

▷ **Gamma Ray**

Fresh from the fire of nuclear reactions, I'll fry you to a crisp. I'm mean, keen, and raring to go. With Speed of Light aiding my travel, I cut right through any material as if it weren't there. It  takes a great thickness of Lead to stop me. I'm extremely dangerous and can hurt humans. It's not all destruction, though—I also have my uses in sterilizing food and killing cancers.

▪ **Gamma Ray Burst**

Can't stop, I'm too energetic! I'm a beam of Energy released by Supernova. In a few seconds I send out more Energy than Sun can shine out in ten billion years!

▷ **Galaxy**

Containing many billions of stars, I swirl around like an island in the vastness of space. My shape tells a story about how I formed—and hints at how I might end.

▷ **Gas**

I fizz, bubble, and pop —I literally hum with Energy. Freed from the tiresome bonds that bind Solid and Liquid, my particles dart around like hyperactive bees.

▪ **Galileo Galilei (1564–1642)**

Galileo Galilei was the godfather of modern science. About 400 years ago, he used the best telescope of the day to peer dimly into Solar System. He tried to prove that the planets orbited Sun and not Earth. The Italian scientist also invented an early version of Thermometer, and studied the way things fall and how Pendulum swings.

I'll disappear right before your eyes, dispersing into thin air. I can be a color, but mostly I'm invisible. My unconfined nature means that I fill any container that I'm put into. Squeeze me into a can and Particle bashes against the sides, exerting Force felt as Pressure. Heat me up and Particle moves around faster, building more Pressure. Squeeze me hard and I'll turn into Liquid if I am cool enough.

◼ Gear

My friends and I are Wheel's rough-edged cousins, engaging little dudes with fine teeth. We are all about connecting up and giving a machine some drive. Here's how we operate: the teeth of one gear interlock with those of other gears to build a tight-knit team called a gear train. We change the direction of spinning components and make them run faster or slower. When one gear spins, the next one locks on and turns as well—but in the opposite direction. If the second gear is bigger, it turns more slowly than the first. If it's smaller, it whirls all the faster.

◼ Gel

Neither Liquid nor Solid, I am something in between. Jelly-like, I am a type of Colloid where Solid is dispersed in Liquid.

▷ Gene

Are you clumsy, like your dad? Tone deaf, like your mom? Blame little old me. I'm a how-to guide for the human body—a code for the instructions for making, running, and maintaining body parts. I'm crucial to your appearance and natural abilities, because Cell uses me to build parts such as Brain, Skin, Hair, and Eye. I come in pairs—one set from Mom and one from Dad.

I'm unbelievably tiny: Inside Cell Nucleus are 46 strands of DNA, tightly curled up. These are called chromosomes. They contain about 20,000 of me! Small sequences of DNA signal the end of one gene and the start of another so that Chromosome can be understood—just as a capital letter and a period give sense to sentences. *Gene*-ius!

◼ Gene Pool

Gather round, all of you. I'm the sum total of all the genes among us. The closer related you are to each other, the smaller I get.

▷ Genetic Modification

I'm a remix master. My specialty lies in stripping out sections of DNA from one organism and knitting it into the DNA fabric of another. Scientists use me when they want to take a desirable trait from one organism and put it into another. I'm used to make better, stronger crops and to turn Bacterium into a mini medicine factory.

G

▷ **Genome**

I am a central library housing all the knowledge needed to completely describe Organism. Contained in my depths are all of Gene's codes and instructions, and a raft of noncoding sequences of DNA, to boot. The 3.2 billion code symbols in the human genome would fill 5,000 books like this one.

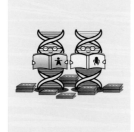

■ **Genotype**

I'm the combination of genes that the cells of a particular individual have. Those genes get together to build a body, and the finished product is called a phenotype.

▷ **Geoengineering**

Bold and ambitious, I am a schemer and a dreamer. One of my master plans is to alter the whole planet to stop Climate Change in its tracks. I propose two lines of attack. The first is to reduce Carbon Dioxide. The second is to lower the amount of sunlight reaching Earth. I can use carbon storage to tuck CO_2 away in nooks and crannies.

Feeding Ocean with Iron would cause a bloom in photosynthesizing Plankton, which sucks up Carbon Dioxide as it grows. Space mirrors—giant reflective sails in orbit around Earth—would bounce away sunlight, while sulfate dust injected into Atmosphere could mimic Volcano's cooling effects. But these harebrained notions are extreme, and their side effects could be worse than the problems they are solving!

■ **Geology**

Geology is the most down-to-earth of all the sciences and lets you get your hands dirty. Rock and Mineral—found mostly beneath our feet—hold all of Earth's secrets. Understanding where Rock came from and how it formed helps scientists answer questions about how Earth fits in with Solar System, how long it has been here, and how we came to live on it. The grandfather of geology, Charles Lyell, suggested that Rock-making processes that happen on Earth today must also have operated in the same way, and at the same rate, in the past.

■ **Germination**

Has spring sprung? If so, it's time for me to sprout. I'm the process that makes Seed grow Root, Stem, and Leaf to make a plant.

G

▷ Glacier

I am made of snow that fell faster than it could melt. I clothe Earth's polar and mountain regions in gleaming whiteness. Be careful, though—it's a whiteness that can make you go "snowblind." In fact, I'm so reflective that I bring Temperature down by beaming sunshine straight back into space! It's an effect called "radiative cooling."

In some places (Greenland and Antarctica, for example), I formed over many thousands of years, snowfall by snowfall. I preserve a record of Climate as it used to be, all locked up in my icy layers. Each year, I grow during the chilly winter months and melt in the summer. I also lose ice by calving— releasing huge icebergs into Ocean. When the globe warms, I melt and sea levels rise. Drip, drip, drip . . .

G

▷ Glands

We are a jolly bunch of squidgy body parts. Our job is to pump Hormone into Blood to speed and slow body processes. We include the thyroid, pituitary gland, and Pancreas.

▷ Gluon

I'm the glue that gums quarks to protons and neutrons, deep inside Atom's nucleus, Although I'm extremely strong, I only operate over very short distances.

▷ Glass

I'm the see-through shiner that lights up your day and keeps the rain out. I'm made by melting sand and other chemicals into a red-hot goo that cools hard and smooth.

▷ Gold

I am the world's most wanted Metal. I am the ultimate attention seeker. I'm soft and easy to shape into jewelry, and I resist Corrosion to stay shiny for years.

◾ Golgi Apparatus

Named after Camillo Golgi, the Italian microscope master, I am a bulbous blob-bubbling machine inside Cell. I'm Organelle—made up of layers of folded membrane. It's my job to packet up chemicals in little sacs and send them out of Cell. (Glands use me all the time!) As the sacs merge with Membrane around other cells, they open up, releasing the chemical inside.

◾ Graphene

Just one Atom thick, but super strong and electrically active, I'm the smartest material around. I am made from a sheet of carbon, where the atoms are arranged in hexagons. I could be used in super-slim screens, even smaller Microchip, or woven in layers or rolled into tubes to make stuff tougher than Steel.

G

▷ Grassland

I am the character with one hundred names—a "steppe" above the rest, if you will. Wherever I am found in the world, my Biome is given a different moniker. I roll out across Continent like an enormous carpet, but I'm an in-betweener, forever stuck between Desert and Forest. Not enough rain falls for trees to grow in large numbers, but grasses and smaller plants seem to love me to pieces!

I have two main types. Temperate grassland almost always lacks trees and is found in places where Climate is temperate, such as Argentina and southern Russia. Savanna is found in warmer parts of the world, such as Africa. Trees are scattered here, but there are never enough for Forest to form. As with many biomes, farmland is taking me over.

◾ Gravitational Constant

Call me Big G, everyone does. Isaac Newton found he needed me when he was linking Gravity to Mass. A bigger mass produces a bigger pull of gravity—but how much more? Add me to the calculations to get an exact result. A century after Newton, Henry Cavendish measured my value. I'm not very big at all—6.6 divided by 100 billion, in fact.

◾ Gravitational Wave

I am the shudders through space itself. Any object with mass—Star, Planet, you name it—can bend space. That leaves warps in its wake like a speedboat on Lake—and those ripple out across space. That's me, and here I come! Astronomers have just figured out how to detect me, and I could reveal things that were otherwise invisible.

▷ Graviton

I'm a shadowy particle, a Boson that carries Gravity through space—maybe. I'm so weak that detectors cannot find me. Hey, I might not even exist!

▷ Gravity

I'm really attractive, and my field of operations is the vastness of space. I hold Earth together, keep the planets in their orbits, and make Star form, as well as more mundane tasks, such as keeping your feet on the ground. I am the weakest of the Fundamental Forces but work over the longest distances.

▷ Greenhouse Effect

I'm a hothouse flower. Without me, Earth's warmth would be lost to space every night, making the planet so cold you'd freeze. No sir, I keep Earth at a comfortable 59°F (15°C), on average, instead of a glacial 0.4°F (−18°C).

When Sun's glowing beams hit Earth, both land and sea absorb Energy from them. Earth heats up and radiates Heat back into Atmosphere. Hanging out in Atmosphere's multilayers are the members of the Greenhouse Gas gang. These guys have molecules that absorb the heat radiation coming from Earth. They act like an extra blanket, making Atmosphere nice and snug.

▷ Greenhouse Gas

I belong to a bubbly bunch that includes Carbon Dioxide, Methane, Nitrous Oxide, and Ozone, among others. Thanks to our ability to absorb Infrared's radiation, we keep Earth toasty and Life moving on.

The problems start when there are too many of us in Atmosphere. We absorb that hothead, Heat, and beam it back to Earth, making the planet hotter. Worse still, our numbers are boosted by human activities, such as burning Fossil Fuel and chopping down Forest, which are contributing to troublesome Climate Change.

G

81

▷ **Habitat**

Earth is infested with a huge number of Life's different forms, and they all need somewhere to live. They have invaded every nook and cranny, from Mountain's highest

top to the deepest of Ocean's trenches. These places are different examples of me, each presenting Life with a certain set of challenges. Should Organism fail any one of my tests, it will not survive.

I influence Evolution, with Species constantly changing (albeit very slowly) to make sure it is best equipped to survive in its own particular patch of the world.

■ **Hadron**

As subatomic particles go, I am a big one. I am made from quarks bonded together. If there is one quark and one antiquark, I'm Meson. If there are three quarks, I'm Baryon, which includes Proton and Neutron.

▷ **Hail**

A real bruiser, I hammer on roofs and strip crops bare. I form in tall storm clouds, where strong updrafts shoot Water's droplets up into Air. Layers of ice build around each drop, and so I

am born! Up, up I go, growing bigger and meaner with each new coat of ice. Once I'm too heavy for the updraft to support me, I plummet all the way down to Earth . . . and destruction.

▷ **Hair**

Face it, I've got you covered! I'm all over you. I offer protection (as eyelashes) and warmth (as scalp and body hair).

I'm a softie, but I'm also very tough—I'm made of the protein keratin and am stronger than a copper wire of the same thickness. I grow slowly and can reach 20–32 inches (50–80 cm) long (as head hair) before falling out. That means your oldest hairs are three to five years old and is why you find so many in the drain! Hair today, gone tomorrow!

■ Half-life

My clock's always ticking. I'm the time it takes for Radioactive Decay to destroy half of a substance. It will take the same time to halve again, so I'm a good measure of how radioactive something is. Frantic francium has a half-life of just 22 minutes—it does not hang around for long. Uranium has a half-life of about 4.5 billion years, and that means there is half of it left from when Earth formed.

■ Halogen

I belong to a caustic killer team from the far-right side of Periodic Table. This is where nonmetal elements live, of which we are the most reactive. Our close-knit group is a feisty one, and our members react violently with Metal to form salts (halogen means "salt maker"). Fluorine and chlorine, the elements at the top of the group, are toxic gases. Next comes bromine, which is a liquid with a terrible stench, and solid Iodine. Astatine, our final member, is so rare and radioactive, no one has ever seen it.

▷ Heart

Stop! Listen! That lub-dub lub-dub you hear is me beating out the rhythm of your life. Some 1,850 gallons (7,000 L) of Blood pump through me every day. I sit at the center of your chest and am about the size of a fist. With each double pump, my right side pushes oxygen-poor Blood out, and from all over the body, to Lung. At the same time, my left side jets oxygen-rich Blood from Lung around the body. Beat that!

▽ Heat

I'm hot stuff, pure and simple, and one of Energy's main forms. I'm Motion on the tiniest scale and Power inside an engine. As particles move faster, zinging around and crashing into each other, they give off Infrared's radiation. You can't see it, but Skin can feel it. When I get really hot, Atom gives off Light and that you *can* see. That's why hot Metal glows and burning Gas flickers as flaming Fire.

In Solid, I shuffle along by conduction. Hot, fast atoms smash into cool, slow ones, making them speed up and heat up. Before you know it, I'm all over the place. In Liquid and Gas, I use convection: hot liquid rises up and cold liquid sinks down to take its place. That cold supply warms up and rises and around I go, again and again.

H

▷ Helium

I am a "noble" gas, so I rarely get involved with the riff-raff elements. I am produced by Star, who uses Fusion to make me from Hydrogen. Radioactive Decay can also make my nucleus—better known as Alpha Particle. I'm very lightweight, so you'll find me in balloons and blimps. I'm also used to super cool Superconductor.

Herbivore

Quick, I don't have much time before my next meal. I'm an animal that eats only plant foods. Plants are full of Vitamin and Mineral, but much of it is hard to digest (especially Leaf). I have to eat a lot of it to get by, and that takes time. I'm normally a big beast with a roomy stomach and intestines to extract the most from my dull diet.

Hermaphrodite

During my life I see it all. I can start out as one sex, such as Male, and then transform into Female as I get older. Many fish use this system. I can also be Male and Female at the same time! I can't mate with myself, but I can be a mother and father all at once. Snails, slugs, and Worm do this.

Hertz

I get a real buzz out of all the ups and downs. I'm the unit for measuring Frequency, and one of me (1 Hz) equals one of Wavelength per second.

▽ Heterotroph

Yum! I'm the great consumer. Unlike Autotroph, I'm not big on building food out of sunshine and chemicals. I'm a fast-food fan on a "see-food" diet—I see food and I eat it! Gulp! Like all living things, I need Carbon to construct my body and keep it running. I get it ready-made from Autotroph.

Autotroph may keep the whole show on the road, sure, but what a dull place it would be without me—I'm talking lions and starfish, grizzlies and mushrooms. As well as plant-nibbling and meat-munching animals, my number includes single-celled Bacterium aplenty. Those minimarvels perform a vital function—they live on the products and remains of organic things, decomposing waste. That's right, it's me that stops the planet from drowning in its own filth.

H

▷ Higgs Boson

Extremely shy and retiring, I played hide and seek with the greatest minds in physics for almost 50 years. My job is to give mass to some particles. Without my effects, Universe would be dull and empty . . . and very warm.

Scientists built a "mass"-ive machine in a bid to capture me—the hugely expensive, proton-smashing, Large Hadron Collider (LHC) in Switzerland. They figure that I appear as a quantum field, which spreads across all of space, clustering around particles of Matter and giving them Mass. Like wading through thick syrup, some particles pick up more of me and move more slowly. It's funny how something as tiny as me could give Mass to anything, but I do explain why some things have more of it than others and why Mass is always positive.

▷ HIV

I'm a ball of badness. People who have me in their bodies are "HIV-positive," but there's nothing positive about me. I lay waste to Immune System by attacking the very defense forces that fight invaders. I kill slowly, often taking several years, in which time I can spread. As yet, there's no cure for me, although there are drugs that slow me down.

■ Homeostasis

Everything in balance is my watchword. I'm a central job of a body, to keep the conditions inside stable and unchanging.

▷ Hormone

I belong to a bustling bunch of errand boys, your body's chemical messengers. Released by Glands, we whiz around your body activating, stimulating, and regulating all kinds of activity.

Need more zip in your heels? We know where to get it. Feeling the stress of a situation? We've got just the thing to help you cope. We get a bad press from teens, whose behavior gets blamed on us, but it's all part of growing up! Take a look at what we do. We regulate Metabolism and manage Energy and your sleep patterns. Homeostasis would be nothing without us.

Horsepower

Early engineers needed a way to describe how powerful their engines and mechanical inventions were. They decided to compare their power to the horse, which did all the work back then. One horsepower is enough to keep 100 low-energy light bulbs glowing.

Hour

I'm the unit of time that can really fly by or drag on for ages. I'm always made up of 60 minutes, or 3,600 seconds. There are 24 of me in a day and night, which is a strange number, but you can blame the ancient Egyptians. They split daylight into ten equal units and then added two more for the twilight time at dawn and dusk. That made 12 of me a day, and so it's only fair that there are an equal number for the night as well.

▷ Hubble Space Telescope

Hubba-hubba. I'm a complete hunk! Flying in low-Earth orbit and shaped like a flip-top trash can the size of a school bus, I've been sent to take snapshots of space without any background light or pesky twinkles produced by atmospheric wobbles.

My beady eye has spied stuff all around Milky Way, but I've made my name by looking outside of Galaxy. Peering into the depths of space, I've been able to look back in time, because Light takes many, many years to travel from distant galaxies. I capture Light from galaxies 13 billion light-years away—the furthest ever seen—showing astronomers Universe as it looked way back then. I'm getting old now, and a new scope, the James Webb Space Telescope, is coming soon to see even farther.

Humidity

Time to get a little bit steamy—or a lot. I'm here to describe how much water vapor is in Air. If I'm high, it will rain soon for sure.

▷ Hurricane

I'm angry Air, chasing my tail, and my might is truly awesome! I form out at sea when Sun evaporates colossal quantities of water off the surface. The rising air and condensing water

vapor build up an enormous swirling cloud. Around and around I go, causing havoc and uprooting anything in my path. When I hit land, wind and Flood can cause disaster.

H

▷ Hydrocarbon

I'm a slick mix of combustible chemicals in Crude Oil and sorted out by Fractional Distillation. I'm a supply of Fossil Fuel and am "cracked" up into other valuable chemicals. I'm made of Hydrogen and Carbon. Simple versions are gases, but melting and boiling points increase as the number of carbons in the chain goes up.

■ Hydroelectricity

The clue is in my long name. I make Electricity in a clean, green way by using the flow of River to spin generators.

▷ Hydrogen

A petite package, I am the simplest and lightest of all the elements, the most abundant in Universe, and the source of everything in it, from Matter and Energy to Life. I'm what fuels Star's nuclear fusion, and I'm the building block for all of Periodic Table's elements.

On Earth, I exist as Gas made up of two hydrogen atoms (H_2). Things go with a bang when I meet Oxygen and Heat. I'm highly flammable. I was once used to fill airships, but a few fatal explosions ended my career. In the future, I will be important in Fuel Cell—a clean and efficient way of generating Electricity.

▽ Hydrothermal Vent

I occur where Earth's undersea tectonic plates are moving apart. Seabed rocks are saturated with Water. Below them, Heat from deep inside the planet blasts Water out of cracks to form my tall mineral-rich chimneys. I am home to the only animals on Earth not sustained by Sun's energy. There are weird blind crabs and shrimp, bright-red giant tubeworms, huge clams, and Pompeii worms—Earth's most heat-tolerant complex animals—sitting very comfortably in Water as hot as 176°F (80°C) or as cool as 68°F (20°C).

■ Hypothesis

I'm an idea that needs to be tested. A scientist thinks me up to explain a mystery and then devises an experiment to prove me wrong or right.

H

I
J
K

▷ Ice Cap

Covering the poles and northern Greenland, I keep Water locked up in an icy blanket. But as Earth grows warmer, I look set to melt, which could spell disaster.

▽ Igneous Rock

Making up 95 percent of Earth's crust, I start out as Magma—liquid rock deep within Earth. Mostly I cool slowly in vast, mountain-size lumps deep underground, making big-crystalled blingsters like Granite. Sometimes Magma reaches the surface, spilling out of Volcano as Lava. Here, Mineral cools quickly, making tiny crystals in rocks like Basalt.

▷ Ice Age

An icy blast from the past, I occur when Earth moves a little farther from Sun, every 100,000 years or so.

I force chilly Glacier and Sea Ice to spread out from the polar regions. I blanket the land in snow and cover the sea in ice. Glaciers grow down mountainsides, carving out valleys beneath them. All that frozen water stuck on land makes the sea level drop by 300 ft. (100 m). To survive during the last ice age, many creatures grew shaggy coats. The snowball Earth theory suggests that an ice age more than 650 million years ago completely froze the whole planet, Ocean and all.

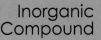

■ Immune System

I run a highly trained special ops team that tracks down invaders in your bloodstream. You know the sort: Bacterium, nasty germs, Virus, and Parasite—utter filth, all of 'em. Always on patrol, B-Cell spots foreign bodies encountered in the past and marks them with Antibody. Then killer T Cell moves in to finish the job. Immunity with impunity, that's my motto!

■ In Vitro

I literally mean "in glass," and I refer to processes that normally happen inside bodies being carried out in laboratories, using high-tech—often Glass—equipment.

■ Induction

Wanna see some magic? I'm as close as science gets. Move Conductor through Magnetic Field and I will make Electricity. This is how Generator works to make Current.

▷ Inertia

Why is everything such a huge effort? You know, why do we have to use Force all the time to get things moving? Well, it's because of me. You see, all Matter has a piece of me— the bigger the Matter, the more of me there is. I keep Matter doing what it has always done, and this only changes if Force flexes a muscle. Even then I put up a fight! I know I cause problems, but without me Motion would be impossible.

■ Infinity

You'll never pin me down. I'm beyond what you can even begin to imagine. Think of a big number, add one, add a million, double it. Whatever the size, there is always a bigger number, and there will be forever. That's my big idea. I'm all the numbers. You can't count on me because I have no end. I'm not a number—you can't use me to add or multiply or do the other things you do with numbers. By the way, my symbol is written like this: ∞. It's a closed double loop with no start and no end—just like me.

▷ Infrared

Invisible to human eyes, I'm given off by hot things. Even in the dark of the night, my telltale signature shines through. Night-vision goggles use me to help people see in the dark. But I can also be used to save people—thermal-imaging cameras are used by rescue services looking for anyone trapped in rubble.

■ Inheritance

I'm the chip off the old block, the reason why a child resembles its mother and father. I use Gene to carry my all-important information from parent to child.

■ Inorganic Compound

Organic compounds come from Life and are built around Carbon. I make up everything else—such as Rock and Mineral.

I

J

K

▷ Insect

A six-legged critter, I belong to the biggest gang of arthropods. We are masters of air and land. Salty Ocean is the only place we don't thrive, but we're working on it! There is more to us than buzzy wasps that spoil a picnic or vibrant butterflies that flit around the yard. Many of us are hidden from view: beetles toil in the soil, busy ants labor underground, and cockroaches lurk in mucky garbage dumps.

■ Insulator

Ye shall not pass! I block the path of Electricity or Heat, which is the opposite of what Conductor does. Mostly I am made from Plastic or Ceramic, and my main job is to shield people from dangerous Current. That is why I'm wrapped around wires and cover plugs and switches. I'm not perfect, of course. Give Charge a large enough push, thanks to Voltage, and Electricity will force itself right through me. Ouch!

■ Internal Combustion Engine

I'm an engine that burns fuel inside (internal combustion, geddit?). Earlier steam engines burned their fuel in a furnace outside the engine. The fuel makes a series of small explosions, and Pressure uses these mini-blasts to push on one or more pistons, making them go up and down—hello, Motion! But hold on, Wheel goes around, not up and down. This magic switch is made using a crankshaft (basically Wheel's axle in a zigzag shape), which puts Motion in a spin.

▽ International Space Station

Cruisin' at 240 mi. (390 km) above Earth, I'm like a diamond in the sky. At $150 billion so far, I'm the most expensive science project ever. I'm a bustling space hub, constructed piece by piece over more than ten years. I'm built on a long truss bolted together in space. Off this structure hang double-sided, Sun-tracking solar arrays that provide power, temperature-regulating radiators, living quarters, and laboratories.

Life is buzzing with plenty of experiments to fill a ten-hour working day. Astronauts stay for up to six months, breathing stale air and drinking (ahem) "recycled" water, eating ready-made dinners, and sleeping tethered to a metal wall. However, they do get to see 15 magnificent sunrises and sunsets every day. Beat that, ground-lubbers!

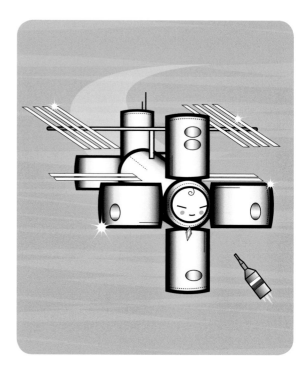

I
J
K

▷ Intestines

I'm your body's food-processing plant, sucking all the juicy goodness from the mush that Stomach passes on. It all starts in my upper part, the small intestine.

I take bile from Liver and Enzyme from Pancreas to mix everything up into a salty broth. My twists and turns are lined with little finger-like villi. They wave around in the slop and the slime, soaking up nutrients, which seep through my walls into Blood. What's left moves on to my farty parts—the large intestine—where I lap up leftover Mineral and Water. There's little wastage, I can tell you! But you already know what is left over.

▷ Invertebrate

Although you think of me, and those like me, as spineless simpletons, we rule the world. My kind make up 97 percent of all animal species on Earth!

We include everything from tiny Plankton floating in the sea to giant squids, the original sea monsters that grow longer than most boats. In between are all sorts of soft jellies, slimy worms, and creepy-crawlies. Some of us, such as some mollusks and Echinoderm, are hard cases who are locked up in shells—for life! Our largest group is armor-plated Arthropod. For our size we beat Vertebrate hands down—even though we don't have any hands, of course. We have world-beating jumpers and weightlifters, and we hold the world land-speed record, too. Beat that!

▷ Iodine

Appearances can be deceptive. I am a shiny black solid, but at room temperature I can change into a purplish gas—without stopping to become a liquid (Sublimation can tell you more). You'll almost never see me alone—I hang out in pairs as a gas.

I am deadly to Bacterium when I'm combined with other chemicals. Then I am a yellow-brown liquid that stings like heck when it gets dabbed onto an open wound. I'm also used to clean up inside the body after surgery. I've been sneaking into people's diets for years in table salt.

I

J

K

▷ Ion

Let's get this party started! It's fine to admire Atom's steadiness, but you want a bit of spark and pizzazz in your chemistry set.

No lone Atom, aside from the elements in Group 8 (see Periodic Table), has a full electron shell. In chemistry, my trick is to transfer Electron to or from the outer shells to fill them up. This creates positively and negatively charged ions—they go by Cation and Anion, respectively. Opposites attract, remember, and that makes for exciting Chemical Reaction! I join positive metal and negative nonmetal ions together in a tight embrace with Ionic Bond. The "ionic compounds" like Salt are rock-solid, with high melting and boiling points. Their brittle crystals often dissolve in Water, and they conduct Electricity when molten.

■ Ionic Bond

Hold it, I'm feeling a strong attraction. I'm the bond that holds ions together. Covalent Bond and I make chemistry what it is.

▷ Iron

I am at the center of everything. As the main element in Blood's hemoglobin, the substance that transports Oxygen around the body, I keep you alive. Journey to the center of Earth and you'll find me right there, inside Core. I am the most abundant Element on Earth, and when used to make Steel, I'm at the heart of engineering, too.

▷ Island

Give me some space! Surrounded by Water, I prefer to stand alone in splendid isolation. I can be big, like Madagascar, or a tiny dot of Rock. It doesn't matter, as long as I'm separated from any mainland by a decent-size body of Water. Canals and River don't count, or else much of Brazil and Venezuela would be islands, too!

■ Isomer

I really shape up. I'm one version of Molecule that contains the same atoms as another version, only they are arranged in a different way.

I
J
K

▽ Isotope

Like the ghastly creation of some crazed scientist in a sci-fi movie, I am Atom's monstrous brother. With the same number of protons as my atomic sibling, I have the same chemistry and undergo the same reactions. However, I have a different number of neutrons in my nucleus—sometimes more, sometimes less.

This unhealthy number of neutrons can give me a nasty streak. Atom tends to be stable, while my unbalanced nucleus can collapse with Radioactive Decay, leaving new elements. Medicine makes good use of Radioactive Decay, but I am most famous for my destructive power: Radon's isotopes in Granite give people cancer, while uranium-235 and plutonium-239 are the active ingredients in nuclear weapons.

▷ Jellyfish

I may be 98 percent water, but I am not a drip! Some of my type are almost invisible, others have a sting in their tails. We float rather than swim, going wherever Ocean's currents take

us. Your best chance of seeing us is when we crowd together in a bloom. This is when our larvae suddenly mature into full-blown jellies, creating an instant swarm of hundreds of thousands of beautiful bobbing blobs.

■ Joint

Sing with me: shin bone connected to the knee bone, knee bone connected to the thigh bone . . . I'm sure you know the rest. I'm the smooth, soft touch that makes all those bone-on-bone connections. There are three types. Sutures are real stiffs. They bond Bone together but cannot move at all. You'll find several of them in Skull. Cartilage links inflexible joints like those linking Spine's bones. Finally, synovial joints bend to your will. The connecting bones are cushioned with soft pads and slung together with Ligament. Muscle is my mover and shaker, allowing me to move in at least two directions—in the case of wrist joints, several directions at once.

■ Joule

N R G, you see what I'm sayin'? I'm the complete unit, measuring Energy of any kind —in Motion, Electricity, or even Sound.

■ Jungle See Rainforest

I

J

K

▽ Jupiter

I could have been a contender—a real star—but instead I'm just the biggest planet. I'm absolutely gigantic, made almost entirely of Hydrogen (plus a little Helium), and I have a system of moons orbiting me. If I'd had just a little bit more beef, I would have burst into life as bright and wonderful Star.

Even though I'm called the King of the Solar System, I'm still angry. I spin rapidly, whirling Atmosphere into thick bands of double-decker clouds that give me my coffee-and-cream appearance. There's nothing genteel about these cloud banks—inside some of them, winds blow at 260 mph (420 km/h), whisking up enormous storms. My most famous blemish—the Great Red Spot—is a storm three times bigger than Earth that's been raging since at least the 1600s.

■ Juvenile

Bottoms! Poop! Oh sorry, you're right. I should grow up. I'm an animal that is not a baby—no way, not me—but not quite an adult yet.

■ Kelvin

Proper science uses Temperature's proper scale. Me. I start at Absolute Zero and can measure a cup of coffee or Star's core.

▷ Kerosene

I'm a fuel that is a little thick and not that sparky, but when I get alight? Man, I burn hot. Pilots use me to reach for the sky, because I release enough Energy for jet engines.

▷ Kidney

I'm one of a pair who cleans up your bloodstream, passing Waste on to Bladder. You'll find us nestled on either side of Spine, enjoying the protection of its ribs.

Over the course of any one day, we filter Blood around 25 times! Think about it, we spend our entire lives soaked in the ruddy stuff. All the fun takes place in microscopic mini-filters called nephrons. Each of us contains about one million of these guys. They squeeze Water and Waste out of Capillary and whisk it swiftly down garbage chutes to Bladder.

I
J
K

◼ Kilo-

I'm a metric system add-on that gives an enormous boost. Wherever I'm seen I denote a thousand-fold increase. Kilogram—1,000 grams; kilometer—1,000 meters. You get the idea, I make it easy when you know how.

◼ Kilowatt Hour

A mash-up of Power and Time, I'm used to explain how much power a home is using. One of me (1 kWh) is equal to using 3.6 million joules. A 10-watt light bulb uses one of me in 100 hours.

◼ Kinesthesia

I'm a spooky sense you probably did not know you had. I use hundreds of body sensors to track your position and posture.

▷ Kinetic Energy

I am the buzz that speed freaks chase. I'm what happens when Mass gets in Motion. I adore Acceleration—as a thing picks up Speed, it gains kinetic energy. Skydivers falling out of the sky can almost feel their potential energy changing into me by the second as the ground rushes toward them. The parachute will cut me down to a safe size before it's too late!

I'm used to make Electricity and power all kinds of machines. All this gusto can come at a cost, though. I'm the one who kills people in a car crash because I depend on Speed squared—travel twice as fast and you have four times as much of me. I am genuinely hot stuff. The hotter an object gets, the more kinetic energy its molecules gain and the more they jostle around.

◼ Kingdom

I am a large group used to classify Life. It used to be just the animal and plant kingdoms, but now there are kingdoms for Bacterium, Fungus, Protist, and Archaea.

▷ Kuiper Belt

My name rhymes with "wiper," but you'd struggle to mop me up. Banished far away from Sun's comfort, I form a wide scattering of frosty missiles. I include many small bodies with a similar makeup to Dwarf Planet. Perhaps you have seen our first close-ups from the New Horizons probe?

I

J

K

L

▷ Lake

Serene and calm, I'm a watery type who prefers peace and quiet. Sometimes the wind stirs me up, but I am rarely bothered by troublesome Tide. I like to lie low in Earth's hollows and nooks, surrounded on all sides by land. Sometimes I am even found in large underground wells, call "aquifers," which are tapped to provide nice cold drinking water.

I am kept full by streams and rainy runoff, and I drain out into River. This cycle keeps me fresh, but if Sun evaporates Water and leaves behind all the dissolved salts and Mineral, then you can call me Brackish.

▷ La Niña

I nearly always follow El Niño but have almost the opposite effect. While El Niño often reduces India's monsoon rains, I tend to swell them, causing floods in Australia. Like El Niño, I am a "natural" weather pattern. I occur every three to six years and can last up to three years. With me around, Temperature drops by as much as 9°F (5°C) in the eastern Pacific Ocean. Blowing strong east-to-west winds across the Pacific, my main activity is to boost Hurricane's power in the North Atlantic. What a naughty girl!

■ Lactose

I'm found in milk, some people find me hard to digest. I am a sugar made from galactose and glucose—a double sugar, in fact. That makes me one of Disaccharide's clan.

▷ Laser

Zap! Pow! I'm razor-sharp, a vision of the future. My industrial lasers and scalpels offer the very latest in cutting-edge Technology.

Unlike Light produced by bulbs, mine is strictly a single frequency, which means I produce one color only. In me, Light's rays are rigidly organized, too, with all the photons in step. This is why I make direct beams, instead of spreading out. I am created inside a lasing medium, which can be solid crystals, semiconductors, or gases. The medium is pumped with Electricity to excite it into producing Light, and there I am!

■ Latent Heat

I'm the energy needed to break bonds to make Solid melt and Liquid boil.

▷ Latitude

I am the planet's greatest all-arounder. My horizontal lines hug Earth, forming big hoops around the globe. Super-long Equator is my most famous line, but I have four significant

others. Between sweltering-hot tropics and the Arctic and Antarctic circles, there are the temperate zones. In hand with Longitude, I let you pinpoint your location with devastating accuracy.

■ Lava

Sticky and hot, I'm molten Magma that has leaked out into the open. Cool it. That's what I do, and become Basalt.

■ Lavoisier, Antoine (1743–1794)

Dubbed the father of chemistry for good reason, Antoine Laurent Lavoisier realized that one part of Air—he named it Oxygen—combined with Hydrogen (he named that, too) to make Water. Another of his fundamental findings was also simple: what goes in to Chemical Reaction always weighs the same as what comes out.

■ Laws of Motion

Isaac Newton laid down us three laws:
1: Nothing moves unless pushed by Force, and it will only stop if Force pushes it again.
2: To reach a certain velocity in a certain time, the heavier something is, the harder Force has to push, and the harder it pushes, the faster the object accelerates. 3: Whenever Force pushes on something, it pushes back in the opposite direction—that is, two Forces are at work.

▷ Lead

Soft and malleable, I'm so easy to work with that the ancient Romans used me for their water-carrying pipes. Over the years, I've gained a bad rep. They say I build up in Bone and

damage kids' development. So now I'm closely regulated. But I am still used as a shield against X-Ray and for roofing.

L

▷ Leaf

It's a tough life being a leaf. My job is to bask in the Sun all day, soaking up as much Light as I can. A plant's food maker, I'm positioned so that I don't block out Light for other leaves,  and I have a wax coat to stop water loss. Because I can't be too heavy, I have a super-light internal frame. I also do a plant's "breathing," absorbing Carbon Dioxide through pores on my surface.

■ Lens

Lend me your eyes. I will reveal the details of a microscopic world and show you objects far beyond what Eye can see. I have a curvy, see-through body, shaped exactly so that Refraction bends Light's beam on to a single point as it shines through me. That is my focus, and it allows me to make small things look big and faraway objects appear nearer.

■ Lepton

I'm a member of Fundamental Particle's family. Along with Quark, I make all Matter, from Atom to more exotic items found only in exploding Star. My leading member is Electron, but there are heavier cousins called muon and tau. I also include a squad of teeny tiny neutrinos. They are very shy but might be the most common type of Matter in Universe—if only you could see them.

■ Leukocyte See **White Blood Cell**

L

▽ Lever

I am the ultimate tool in your kit. I'll lift, hit, and crush all before me. It's my job to transmit Force. When Force is applied at one end (the "effort"), Motion shifts it to the opposite end. Here, Force (now the "load") is much stronger and usually acts in the opposite direction.

My crucial feature is the pivot—my whole world rotates around this point. If my pivot is dead center, your effort is equal to the load. But I love to crank things up. Move the pivot closer to my load end, and a small effort becomes mighty. That's what I'm doing in a car jack—you pump my handle and I'll lift the whole car! I come in three classes—and I'm just about everywhere. Next time you use an oar, a wheelbarrow, or some tweezers, that'll be me in action. Show some Muscle!

■ Levitation

Look, no hands—or feet, or anything. I'm the power to float in midair thanks to Force Field.

▷ Life

I am the mysterious quality that separates lamb from lamb chop —a delicate effect that animates Matter. Scientists struggle to capture my spark. I allow living things to take in Energy and use it to grow; to adapt to changes in the environment; and to make copies of themselves. On Earth, my many forms are all carbon- and water-based beings that are made from Cell.

■ Ligament

Elastic and fantastic, I'm the stretchy bands of Cartilage that link Bone to Bone in Joint.

▷ Light

I'm a very bright, colorful kind of guy. Ha—without me, everything would be completely colorless and dark. You can see me (Eye picks up my special characteristics), but you cannot touch me. I come out of Atom when it has too much Energy. When I hit an object, I might bounce off. You can see those objects because I've reflected off them into your eye.

■ Light-Year

Distances from Star to Star are too much for miles, even Astronomical Unit. Instead please use me, the distance light moves in a year: about 5.88 trillion miles (9.46 trillion kilometers).

▽ Lightning

My bolts heat Air about three times hotter than Sun's surface. Air expands so fast that it breaks the sound barrier and makes Sonic Boom, which you hear as thunder. I spark out of Thunderstorm's turbulence. Water droplets, ice crystals, and dust bump and jostle in winds to create Static Electricity. To discharge, I send out a negatively charged stream of electrically charged Air. A positively charged feeler rises up from any high point on Earth. As soon as the two connect, I discharge with full force. Flash!

L

▷ Limestone

Graceful in sheer white, I form in balmy shallow seas, where calcium carbonate is laid down as soft mud. I am made up of pieces of Coral and seashells of all sizes. When I become solid Rock, I'm long-lived, and I make a good building material. However, I dissolve easily in Acid. Even rain can carve through me, which is why the world's limestone areas are riddled with caves and potholes.

■ Linnaeus, Carl (1707–1778)

The father of modern taxonomy, Swedish botanist Carl Linnaeus (1707–1778) devised the useful system of naming organisms so that each has a two-part name in Latin.

L

▷ Liquid

Nothing much bothers me, man. Like an old-school beatnik, I just go with the flow. If there are obstacles in my way, I work around them, and I change my shape easily to fit into any container you choose.

I am fussy about whom I mix with. Sometimes I slip right in with other liquids, but other times I flat out refuse. You can see this in the Oil's rainbow drops in dirty puddles. Mutual attraction between my molecules causes surface tension, a Force that makes me form drops. I resist being compressed, and I expand when heated. If you heat me up or decrease pressure around me, I'll eventually evaporate away as Gas. When I dissolve Solid, I'm called Solvent.

■ Liquid Crystal

Chemically twisted, when electrified I straighten out. That lets Light pass through. I'm electrified in patterns to light up screens—or keep them dark.

▷ Liver

Wow! Is there anything I can't do? I am a multitasker extraordinaire. I'm a scrapyard for Protein and worn-out Red Blood Cell, and a cleaner that scrubs toxins from Blood. But my specialty has to be Digestion. I process and collect nutrients from Blood, which gets piped in to me from Intestines.

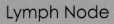
▷ Longitude

I am a straight-up kind of guy. My lines carve up the planet like segments of an orange, cutting through the lines of Latitude at right angles. My lines all meet at the North and South poles. Passing north-south through London, my Greenwich meridian is set at zero degrees. East of the meridian, clocks jump forward. Travel west, and they lag behind.

■ Lovelace, Ada (1815–1852)

Working in the 1840s, this brilliant mathematician was the world's first computer programmer.

▷ Lung

Heave-ho! I am half of a pair of bellow fellows, the inflatables in charge of your body's ventilation. It's a complex task, so take a deep breath—you're gonna need it!

I am a spongy bag made of minute bubble-shaped chambers of the softest, pinkest, foamiest flesh. These are called alveoli, and it is here that Oxygen from Air gets exchanged for Carbon Dioxide. Here's how it works: your windpipe divides many times over inside me and my twin, making millions of microscopic tubes that spread out to all of our alveoli. Capillary carries Blood through the alveoli with Red Blood Cell on board, who picks up Oxygen, ready for transportation to Cell. As Blood does this, it also deposits Carbon Dioxide waste, which you breathe out before breathing in again.

▷ Lymph

I'm a real drip. I'm pale Liquid that oozes out from cuts before they start to bleed. I trickle among Tissue to provide a cleansing service. I'm mostly made of Water and White Blood Cell. As Blood squeezes through Capillary, I filter out via my own lymphatic vessels. Immune System's helpers come along for the ride, looking to combat any invading bugs.

■ Lymph Node

I am like a field hospital, removing the bodies from Immune System's battles. I swell when you are fighting an illness.

L

M

MACHO

My name stands for MAssive Compact Halo Object. I'm a heavy but dark object that hangs around the far edge of galaxies. I'm hard to spot, and astronomers think I might account for some of the missing Dark Matter.

▷ Magma

I'm hot, melted Rock, but you'll always find me underground. It's me that makes most igneous rock. Sometimes I rise to the surface to create Volcano. My molten liquid melts Crust until, eventually, I explode out onto the surface. I'm called Lava the moment I meet Air.

■ Mach Number

Named after Ernst Mach, the scientist who discovered the sound barrier, I show how many times faster than Sound a plane or rocket flies. Mach 1 is the speed of Sound. Space rockets can hit Mach 13 during launch. Boom if you wanna go faster.

▷ Machine

I am a mechanical marvel. If you need a force multiplier, a groovy mover, or a hefty lifter, look no further. I belong to a cool crew whose members transform Energy so that you can get things done, either by redirecting Motion or by controlling Force. We always feature one or more of a simple set that includes Wheel and Axle, Screw, Ramp, Wedge, and Lever. It is this team that makes my clever contraptions fit for the task.

▽ Magnesium

I'm happy to mix in any social gathering of the elements, making friends with many of them, even moody Hydrogen. I am a sparky fellow and I often cause a reaction! I'm also a mischievous sprite—I can speed up your body processes and make you rush to the bathroom! The laxatives Epsom salts and milk of magnesia are both made using my compounds. Chlorophyll relies on having me at its center to perform its fantastic light tricks during Photosynthesis.

I am a silver-white Metal, and I burn with incredible intensity and a bright white light. I work with Combustion to produce the flash in a camera's bulb, distress flares, fireworks, and incendiary bombs. Strong and light, I help make bike frames, car parts, and aircraft engines.

■ Magnetic Field

Invisible but powerful, I'm the spooky dude that pushes and pulls unseen. I'm a field of Force around Magnet, and I'm felt by charged objects, magnets, and certain metals. I'm produced when charged Particle is on the move in Electricity, when Electric Field shifts position, or by Electron moving through a magnetic material.

▷ Magnetism

Proof that opposites attract, among much more, I make Iron's atoms line up to face the same way. Working together, they push and pull on other iron pieces. My magnets have two poles: north and south. Opposite poles pull together, while two the same push each other away.

■ Magnification

If you need more detail, I'll zoom right over. I use Lens to make small objects appear larger (check Microscope to see) and distant objects closer (ask Telescope to show you).

▷ Male

Of the two sexes, I do the least. I provide half of the DNA that Egg needs to make a baby. That's it! Sperm has to act fast, of course, but the rest is up to Female.

M

▷ Mammal

I belong to a diverse bunch that can survive almost anywhere. We all have Hair and give birth to live young. A baby's first meal is milk from its mother.

■ Manganese

I'm a hard and brittle Element. I am found in large amounts in Ocean's rocky floor, and I'm most widely used to make Steel. That toughie is even stronger when it is joined with me. I can exist in many different forms in Compound, and I change my appearance like an undercover agent—I can be pink, black, green, or dark purple.

▷ Mantle

I'm the filling in Earth's planetary sandwich. A goo of Magma with rocky Crust above and red-hot Core below. Watch out, I can tear Crust apart with a mere shrug.

▷ Marble

Waxy and clear, my complexion drives artists and architects wild. I'm made from sedimentary Limestone and come in huge blocks without any layering, which is why I'm great to carve. I'm often formed if cooked by Heat and Pressure, when my grains of calcite become interlocking calcite crystal. You'll see me in fireplaces and tiles.

▷ Mars

Hanging in the night sky like a bloodshot eye, I'm a rusty old warhorse, named after the Roman god of war. Iron minerals give me my reddish, inflamed look. I'm a chilly, hard-bitten world of dead volcanoes and dry rift valleys. Earthlings are fascinated by the idea that I could be home to Martian aliens, yet despite all their probing, there's still no sign.

■ Maser

I'm the bro of Laser. My M is for invisible Microwave, and only later did Laser get better known by giving out Light.

M

▽ Mass

As someone who gives an object its heft, I'm a character of substance, I can tell you. You see, all matter has some of me—from tiniest Atom to enormous Star. This is not true for all "things" though—Energy, Photon, and Gluon (the dude who carries Strong Force) are massless.

The weight of an object is a measure of Force acting upon it. Unlike Weight, however, I don't depend on Gravity, so I never change. For scientists, "massive" doesn't mean huge. Dense things can cram a lot of me into a small space. A teaspoon of Neutron Star, for example, can contain over five trillion tons of me! Objects containing me all have their own alluring force of Gravity, which draws them to each other—and things with a lot of me are very attractive!

■ Mass Number

Atomic Number gives Element its identity, but I'll give a bigger and better picture. I am the total number of particles in Nucleus —that's protons plus the neutrons. This shows how heavy Atom is. (Electron is so lightweight, there is no need to count that.) Thanks to Isotope's variations, not every Atom of one Element has the same Mass Number, so chemists take an average to be accurate.

■ Mass Spectrometer

When chemists need to know what is in a substance, they call me in. I'm a curved vacuum tube fitted with powerful magnetic and electric fields. Chemists fire in electrified Gas at one end. Electric Field zips Molecule and Atom into a beam, and Magnetic Field curves them around my big bend. Lighter stuff bends more than the heavy stuff, so they all hit a target in a specific place. The pattern of hits tells the chemists what chemicals are present.

■ Matter

I'm a light-touch word for a weighty idea. I can be anything that has Mass—so that's every Atom and Subatomic Particle. I also include Dark Matter, which has Mass, but that is all I know about it. I do not include stuff like Light, Heat, and Sound. They matter (a lot) but they are not Matter.

■ Mechanics

As well as being the tough guys and gals who fix up cars, I'm used by scientists to describe the mathematics of Motion. What goes up must come down, sure, but I'll tell you where, when, and how hard.

M

Medium

Okay, I can mean in between or neither big nor small. That is true enough, but in science I have a more precise meaning: I am the substance surrounding Wave. In Ocean's waves, I am Water, and for Sound I can be Air or Rock. Light and other kinds of radiation have no need for me at all, which is weird. Light propagates as vibrations in a force field, which is how it shines through nothing.

Meiosis

Sperm and Egg are cells with a difference. Instead of being a complete copy of an older Cell—for that see Mitosis—they are half versions that are built to work in pairs to produce a new individual (like you, me, and sweet peas). I am the process of cell division that turns Cell, with its full set of DNA, into four "gametes," or sex cells, with half sets of DNA.

I rely on Cell having a double set of DNA to start with: one from Mom and another from Dad. In my two-in-one deal, Cell divides two times over so one becomes four. In the first division, the doubled up DNA is sorted into two groups—each moving to a new cell. In the second division, the two cells split again, making a total of four Sperm or four of Egg.

▷ Melting Point

I'm soft and schmaltzy, and my crooning will melt any Solid's heart. The forces between Atom and Molecule in Solid are strong and stable, so it takes Energy to break them. When you heat up Solid, Particle vibrates more and more until, finally, it has enough internal Energy to break apart. Measure Temperature as Solid turns to mush, and you have found me!

Membrane

Slick and strong, I'm the ultrafine layer of Fat that makes a bag around Cell and Organelle. I'm a barrier to large molecules, but Water and Gas just go right through me.

▷ Mendeleev, Dmitri (1834–1907)

This Russian chemist is the inventor of the periodic table of elements. He had his bright idea for organizing Element while playing the card game solitaire, where you set out cards in rows and columns. Mendeleev replaced cards with elements and Periodic Table was born!

M

▷ Mercury, metal

Quick and deadly, that's me. A sinister, silver-colored killer, I am a strange and stealthy liquid metal that easily vaporizes into toxic fumes. I put the "mad" in the Mad Hatter—hat makers who used mercury nitrate for their work often succumbed to a strange delirium called "mercury madness." My ability to poison Brain is legendary, and most of the forms I take are lethal. I tend to build up inside the bodies of animals, especially in fish that swim in water polluted by me. I attack the nervous systems of those who eat the contaminated fish.

Alchemists thought they could use me to turn cheap Metal into Gold, and I was once used in goldmining, for Tooth's fillings, and in Thermometer. Safety regulations now restrict my use, and I'm difficult to find.

▷ Mercury, planet

I can't hang around. There's no time for admiring the view when you live this close to a burning-hot fireball. I don't stray far from Sun, so you'll only ever catch sight of me around daybreak or nightfall. Like a courier delivering a package, I scoot across the horizon. It's this activity that led the ancient Romans to name me after their messenger god.

My fast-paced lifestyle makes it hard for spacecraft to visit me, and only one side of me has been photographed. I'm not a pretty sight—my rocky surface is pitted and pockmarked with impact craters.

■ Meson

I'm Baryon's lightweight, flighty, and flaky little brother. Let's get the particle patter out of the way. I am a hadron, because I'm built from quarks, but unlike Proton and Neutron, I have just two of them, not three. Weirdly, I'm a little bigger than Proton, but I only hang around a few thousandths of a second. I get mashed up in high-energy smashups such as in Supernova and Cosmic Ray's collisions.

■ Metabolism

Mine is a catch-all term for the thousands of chemical reactions taking place inside Cell right now! My reactions that break up stuff are called catabolic, and those that build you up again are anabolic. I am the stuff of Life itself, all controlled by my teeming team of enzymes.

M

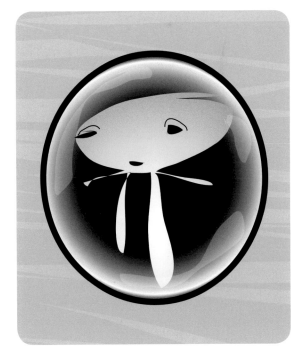

▽ Metal

Your easily persuaded and pliable friend, I make up most of Periodic Table's members, outnumbering Nonmetal by four to one. My chemical and physical properties come from the fact that my outer electrons are not fixed to Atom. Thanks to Metallic Bonding distributing my atoms' electrons, I'm tough stuff that bends but does not break. Sodium, Potassium, and the other "alkali metals" are super reactive.

The transition metals, like Iron and Copper, are more dependable, especially when waltzing along together as Alloy. They are often used in dyes and fireworks, and many belong to Catalyst's gang. However, they all have a weakness for Corrosion. Gold and Silver are more precious about who they mix with, so they stay pure for longer.

M

▷ Metallic Bonding

You'll find me inside Metal, a tough guy whose properties are based on the way I bind Atom. Internally, Metal is arranged into lattices of positive Ion with "seas" of

Electron washing around in between. It's the attraction between Ion and Electron that glues the whole thing together.

■ Metalloid

The best of both worlds, I'm hard and shiny like Metal but brittle like Nonmetal. I may conduct Electric Current, or I may not. Check out Semiconductor for more.

▷ Metamorphic Rock

A mighty morphing shapeshifter, I start out as one type of rock but change when I encounter Heat or Pressure. This can happen when hot

Magma wells up nearby or during periods of Mountain's creation when Earth's huge plates grind into one another.

■ Meteor

Look up, because I always come out of the sky. I'm a "shooting star" that flies through Atmosphere. I arrive from space as Rock and am called a meteoroid when in space.

▷ **Meteorite**

Look out! After blazing through Earth's atmosphere, I smash a crater into the ground. To be one of me, you can't be any old space rock—you have to make it all the way down. Burn up before reaching the ground, and you're just Meteor—a "shooting star." My main claim to fame is being blamed for wiping out Dinosaur. What a meanie!

■ **Meteorology**

I collect up-to-the-minute data from my tracking pals, weather station and remote-sensing satellite, along with Climate's records of its long history. I use the info to make mathematical equations relating to Weather. Then I feed Equation into a supercomputing system.

The more closely Equation matches the real physics of Earth's systems, the more accurately I can predict the future. It's not all good news, I'm afraid: my work shows that Earth's rate of warming is increasing, and that means things could turn nasty.

■ **Metric System**

Invented after the French Revolution as a way of ensuring measurements of Distance, Area, and Weight were always fair, I'm a simple set of units based on the meter, kilogram, and amp. My big innovation was to count up (and down) in tens, hundreds, and thousands. That sounds obvious now, but older measurements are far more complex.

▽ **Microchip**

A little magic box of digital wizardry, I'm made of millions (billions) of tiny electronic gizmos called transistors. Transistor is a traffic-control system for tiny currents of electricity. Bits run the show: 0 switches Current off, and 1 turns it on. Countless switcheroos combine to control Computer according to the millions of bytes in a program.

Transistor is tiny—15,000 of them all lined up would measure just 0.4 in. (1 cm) across — so wiring them up one by one would be impossible. Instead, Transistor and its intricate connections are all etched onto a slice—or chip—of silicon. That's me! I get everywhere these days. I'm inside your smart phone, clocks, credit cards. You'll even find me in ID for lost pets! Chip by little chip, I've changed the way the world works.

M

■ Microorganism

It may look as if big, hairy animals rule Earth, but you live in an age of the Microorganism —a beast so small you need Microscope to spot it. My clan includes tiny cousins Bacterium and Archaea, strange stripped-down Virus, blobby Protist, and teensy members of the Fungus and Algae families. More bacteria loiter in your mouth than there are people on Earth! Some of us are super-hardy—they can survive in the roughest, toughest places.

■ Microscope

I use Magnification to show off details far too small to see with Eye alone. I work when Lens uses bright Light shining on, or through, specimens. More powerful versions of me use Electron's beams.

M

▷ Microwave

I'm Radio Wave's smaller partner, where Wavelength is measured in millimeters. I sit at the top rank of the radio frequency band. I have single-handedly invented a new food industry—the microwave meal! My wavelengths of about 30 mm can excite Molecule in Water, Fat, and sugar—when it feels me, it cannot help vibrating. As Molecule jostles about, its transfers Motion from one molecule to the next, increasing the food's internal Energy and heating it up.

Microwave ovens are shielded by Metal so that I don't cook everything in the kitchen. At other wavelengths I'm much safer, and I'm used in Cell Phone's signals, in spy satellite scanners, and for trapping speeding motorists. But stealth bombers are invisible to me, so they fly right under my prying eyes.

▷ Milky Way

Hanging in space like a gigantic pinwheel, I am the place that Sun and billions of other stars call home. I'm mind-twistingly enormous—100,000 light-years wide.

With Sun buried inside the Orion arm, your view of my huge central bulge is blocked. However, on dark nights, its glare is enough to make a pale stripe of stars across Earth's sky. My lovely big belly is crammed with red and yellow stars. Then, buzzing around in a halo, are tight bunches of ancient stars called globular clusters. They often collide to form superhot blue stragglers. Meanwhile, at my center lies supermassive Black Hole.

▷ Mineral

I belong to a crowd that makes Rock what it is. Without us, that boulder is nothing. We have rules, though. We all need a predictable chemical composition and a definite internal structure. Our members include metals and some of the world's most valuable crystals, plus many that are common as dirt!

■ Minute

In old-timer French I mean "small," and I am the small unit of time—one-sixtieth of an hour, or 60 seconds, if you like.

▷ Mitochondrion

Fast and furious, I'm the little guy who generates Cell's power. And it's no mean feat! I whiz around (there are millions of us) making a fuel called ATP. It's full of life-giving Energy and ready whenever Cell needs some juice. The more Cell wants, the more we make. And when demand threatens to outstrip supply, we simply divide and multiply to increase our output.

■ Mitosis

When new cells are needed, I step in to save the day. I simply divide Cell to produce two new, identical copies.

▷ Mixture

I blend substances together without any of Compound's heated reactions. I'm just a relaxed merging of one substance with another. I'm all mixed up, but each part of me can be separated by physical means. Liquid mixtures are separated using Distillation or Chromatography.

▽ Mole

I am used to count atoms. One mole of atoms is equal to Atomic Mass in grams. For example, the atomic mass of Hydrogen is 1, so 1 mole of hydrogen atoms weighs 1 gram.

M

▷ **Molecule**

There's nothing flash about me. I am a safe pair of hands who lets two or more nonmetals combine, to make electrically neutral, stable substances, such as Water and Nitrogen.

The smallest unit of a compound, I am made by reactions that combine atoms from two or more elements together. Whatever the combination, the atoms always link together to form a specific shape. Most molecules use Covalent Bond to link the atoms together, although this is not always the case. Once I start to break up for any reason, I no longer represent that compound.

M

▷ **Mollusk**

I do my best to look like a tough guy, but inside I am a real softie—and a bit slimy, too (sorry). My relatives are not always obvious—I have snails (one shell) and oysters, and cockles and mussels (two shells) in my clan. Some of us sift food from Water using a snotty net; the rest of us scrape up food with a jagged, iron-rich cutting tool called a radula. The largest (and brainiest) mollusks of all are octopuses and squids. All legs and tentacles, those dudes have no shell at all—other than a thin sliver of one hidden deep inside.

Don't get me wrong—we do have some things in common. Our organs are inside a soft body called the mantle, and we get around using one muscular foot. Most of us live in a watery habitat, but we also glide on to land as long as it is moist enough.

■ **Momentum**

A measurement of Motion, I use Speed and Mass to work things out. I'm always conserved, which means that during a collision, the Momentum on one object is added to that of the other. You can see me at work in a game of pool—I'm passed on when the white ball hits another.

■ **Monomer**

Mono- means "single." My goal is to be linked with my kind into a long chemical chain. That chain is Polymer (poly means "many").

■ **Monosaccharide**

Made from a ring-shaped molecule of five or six carbon atoms, I'm a very simple kind of sugar. Glucose is my most common variety.

■ Month

I sit between Year and Day as a unit of time. I'm based on the Moon, which takes about one of me to go from new moon to half moon to full moon and then back again. Year sees this 12 (or 13) times, and the four lunar stages (half-full-half-new) last a week each. It all adds up.

▷ Motion

If you need to get a move on, just let me know. Thanks to me, the whole Universe is on the move. I work with Force (who always gets me going) to shift objects along and around, up and

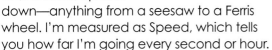

down—anything from a seesaw to a Ferris wheel. I'm measured as Speed, which tells you how far I'm going every second or hour.

▷ Mountain

Distant, magical, cold, and inaccessible, I am a lofty fellow whose head is in the clouds. I snake across the land in belts and chains, like scars on Continent. These lines are the stitch marks where two pieces of Earth's crust have been joined together when tectonic plates collide.

Crust's plates crumpling into one another push Rock up in huge wrinkles that form my longest ranges. The taller and more jagged my peaks, the younger I am, because older ranges have been smoothed out by Erosion. My Himalaya range is still on the up and up. Every year, as the Indian plate piles into Asia, it rises by as much as 0.4 in. (1 cm).

▷ Muscle

I'm a bulked-up, boisterous bodybuilder that makes up about 40 percent of your body weight. My long ropey fibers can only pull in one direction, so I work in pairs. One bunch bends while the other bunch straightens. My length shortens as I pull, which is why I bulge when I tighten.

■ Mutation

I am an error that creeps into DNA when it is copied. Without me, DNA could never change, which makes me an important part of Evolution.

M

▷ Nanoparticle

I live in the realm of the itty-bitty. Forget fleas: things in my world are just atom-wide. I come in an array of dazzling shapes—cuboid, rod, sphere, and banana —that are all 10,000 times thinner than a cat's whisker. Each minuscule Particle has unexpected talents.

Take Silver. It has the natural properties to kill Bacterium and Fungus, whereas a sprinkling of nanosilver acts as a ruthless killer of germs. Why? Because it has much more surface area to its volume, which makes Atom more reactive and powerful. Sometimes it is just our teensy size that makes us special.

▷ Nail

Hard as nails, I am the toughie hangin' off the ends of your fingers and toes. Made from the same stuff as Hair, I pinch, scratch, gouge, prise, dig, and take the knocks life deals us. Your finger judges the hardness of something when you touch it, by pressing up against me. Without me, your rubbery fingertip would bend right back on itself (ouch!).

■ Nanometer

Move aside millimeter, you're crowding me out. I'm one-billionth of a meter, which is useful for measuring Atom and Molecule.

■ Natural Selection

I make Life what it is today—and tomorrow. The best adapted species survive changes to the environment. In so doing, Life slowly, slowly evolves.

▷ Nebula

Nebulae like me are Universe's coldest, darkest places. Out of sight behind our curtains of dust and gas, new stars are born. My clumpy clouds of Hydrogen are swirled into balls of Gas by Supernova or passing Star. Gassy balls fall in on themselves, under their own gravity, to become stars.

▽ Neon

I must be the funkiest Element around. My name is derived from the Greek word *neos*, which means "new." (Maybe any new element could have been christened this way, but I think it suits me very well.) Things really get going when I become excited by electrical energy—Electron zaps and zings and makes me emit brilliant, stunningly colored red Light. The same process can make a whole rainbow of colors if you use different gases, but they are still all called "neon lights" after my pioneering work.

Even though I am found in something as common as Air, I am a member of Periodic Table's aristocracy—the noble gases. I keep myself to myself. I am a colorless, odorless, and tasteless gas, and there is virtually nothing that I will react with.

▷ Neptune

As the farthest true planet from Sun, I am most definitely "out there." Wrapped in a cool blue shroud, I'm Solar System's cold king of bling. Beneath my ice-cold surface lies Ocean, but not as you know it. With boiling methane in its makeup, it glitters with sparkling crystals.

▷ Nervous System

Your sparky communication network, I send signals as electric pulses. I connect Senses to my control center, Brain, and then carry commands to Muscle. My billions of branches cover the entire surface of your body with sensitive nerve endings that detect Touch, pain, and Heat.

▷ Neuron

I am a real live wire, a type of cell that makes up Nervous System. You are, literally, one big bag of nerves. I'm joined together in long chains that connect you up from head to toe. Each one of me has tiny thread-like extensions so I can stay in touch with hundreds of my neighbors.

N

▷ Neutrino

I am a Subatomic maverick. Trillions of my type stream off Sun every second, produced by Fusion in Core. We pass right through Earth without hitting anything.

Over 50 billion neutrinos whiz through your body each second, but you don't feel a thing—with almost no mass and no electrical charge, we're virtually undetectable.

Scientists studying Sun's reactions use vast vats of liquid xenon in deep mineshafts to watch for us. Tiny puffs of Energy in the liquid signal our passing. It took 26 years to find us, and we come in three "flavors."

▷ Neutron

Once Proton had been found at the heart of Atom, something still seemed to be missing. That turned out to be me. Cramped up tightly with Proton, I am a calming influence —without me, the unruly protons would repel each other and fly off.

Along with Proton, I beef up Atom and give it Mass. There are often more neutrons than protons in Nucleus, but sometimes a few more of us squeeze in, making heavier (and often radioactive) Isotope. My name gives the game away. I am entirely uncharged and totally neutral and thus unaffected by Electromagnetic Force. Extract me from Nucleus and fire me at Atom's heart, and Atom might split apart. This causes the violent fission reactions that are used in nuclear power and atomic bombs.

▷ Neutron Star

At only 6 to 12 mi. (9.6 to 19.3 km) across, I'm a tiny star, yet I weigh up to twice as much as Sun. I spin at dizzying speeds, too— once every second is quite slow, don't you know! I'm made of

neutrons that form when Atom is squashed by Gravity. I am normally spotted as a pulsar giving out alien-like bleep signals.

■ Newton

The unit of Force, I'm named after the main man Isaac. One newton (1 N) is the force needed to accelerate 1 kilogram to 1 meter per second in one second.

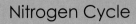

■ Newton, Isaac (1642–1727)

"Genius" is not really strong enough to describe this physicist. He figured out laws for Motion and Gravity in his backyard. He also investigated Light and Heat in his living room and invented calculus, a new kind of mathematics for measuring change.

▷ Nickel

I'm a devil in disguise, often mistaken for Copper. My name comes from the German word *Kupfernickel* ("devil's copper"). I love hanging out with Periodic Table's other transition metal elements, and I'm great at forming Alloy to make materials stronger and resistant to Corrosion. You'll find me in coins, charging around in batteries, and in special heat-resistant materials.

▷ Nitrogen

I'm normally calm, even dull, but I've got an explosive temperament. You might hardly notice me, but I make up almost 80 percent of Air. I'm a pretty unreactive gas, made up of two atoms of nitrogen (N_2) bonded together for safety. The triple bond between these two atoms is hard to break, and that is what lies behind my hidden power.

When Atom forms these bonds, it releases Energy. My compounds put the bang into Explosive. I'm very easy to extract from Air and am a spectacular coolant as Liquid. At close to –330°F (–200°C), I will freeze almost anything that comes into contact with me.

■ Nitrogen Cycle

I represent the element Nitrogen on Earth. My client is essential to Life on that planet, and I make sure everything is getting the supply it needs. Nitrogen is a vital ingredient in a mind-boggling array of compounds—you'll find me in Chlorophyll, DNA, and, most importantly, Amino Acid and Protein. Life cannot just take Nitrogen in from Air like it does with Oxygen. So it is a plant's job to find Nitrogen's compounds in soil.

Farmers add ammonium or nitrate compounds to their fields—Fertilizer, which gives me a boost. My next step is to move the compounds to animals through Food Web as they eat plants (and each other). Bacteria complete me. Some turn dead bodies back into pure Nitrogen, and others "fix" the gas again and add it to the soil.

N

▷ Nitrous Oxide

I am a natural part of Nitrogen Cycle, but with humans spreading Fertilizer on fields and burning Fossil Fuel, my levels in Air are slowly creeping up. This gives me a pretty fearsome reputation as a long-lasting greenhouse gas. I'm over 300 times more effective than Carbon Dioxide.

■ Nobel, Alfred (1833–1896)

This chemist from Sweden invented dynamite and other "safe" explosives. He made a lot of money and used it to create the Nobel prizes, the greatest awards in science.

N

▷ Noble Gas

Periodic Table's far-right-hand side is the classy neighborhood—home to me and my pals. Our gases are noble because they resist almost any involvment with the rest of the elements. We are also called "inert gases," meaning completely unreactive. But this isn't entirely true—some of us have been caught in clandestine clinches with Fluorine and other highly reactive elements.

My group is made of Helium, Neon, Argon, krypton, and xenon. Argon is the most common in Earth's atmosphere, and the others are found in tiny amounts in Air. Krypton (the hidden one) and xenon (the strange one) are gathered for several uses. Both gases are added to Light's bulbs (especially in the headlights of fancy cars) to make them last longer.

■ Nonmetal

I belong to Periodic Table. When it comes to me, Melting Point and Boiling Point are pretty low. I am poor at conducting Heat and Electricity, which is not always a bad thing.

▷ Nose

Deep inside me is a little patch of chemical sensors. Without these, you'd not be able to smell anything or taste your food. But that's not all I do. Tiny hairs snag grime on its way into your body. My mucus mops it up and the hairs sweep the gunk to the back of the throat. "Snot" bad, eh?

▷ Nuclear Energy

I should warn you, I'm very unstable. Keep me under control, and I produce huge amounts of Energy for turning into Electricity. But if you're not careful, I could just go off with an almighty BANG. I come from Atom's tiny, throbbing heart—a cluster of clingy particles with the tightest grip of anything Universe has to offer. If Particle breaks off from Nucleus, it releases a whoosh of Energy. Okay, so Atom doesn't add up to much on its own, but give me a few pounds of the right stuff, and I'll make the biggest explosion you've ever seen.

I only really get going in radioactive materials—overweight atoms where Nucleus just won't sit right. Every now and then Particle breaks off! But watch out, I produce dangerous Radiation. It's a killer!

■ Nucleolus

Electron Microscope is essential if you want to see me. I'm a tiny bagged-up region within Cell Nucleus. I have several jobs to do—in fact, doctors and cell scientists are still drawing up a list. My big role is manufacturing Ribosome, which is sent out into the rest of Cell (especially rough Endoplasmic Reticulum), where it reads the information from DNA held in Nucleus.

■ Nucleon

Sometimes it seems physicists just like to give out names. I refer to any Particle found in Atom's nucleus. There are only two: Proton and Neutron. Remember these are also known as Baryon, as well as Hadron, so I'm a third word used to describe them. I think that is enough for now.

■ Nucleus, Atomic

Hi, can you squeeze in here? There is not much room inside me. I'm the central core of Atom where Proton and Neutron cling together. I hold more or less all of Atom's mass, but I am a thousand trillion times smaller! Yep, you read that right. Strong Force is so strong that it makes me really pull myself together. And so, you see, most of Atom—most of everything—is just empty space.

■ Nucleus, Cell
See **Cell Nucleus**

■ Nutrition

I'm the science of food, and I chew over how much Energy is in meals and what kinds of useful nutrients are included.

N

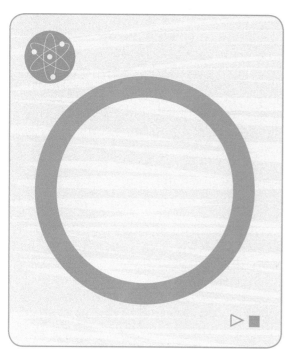

▷ Ocean Wave

Life for me is full of ups and downs! I am created by the wind. The friction of Air against Ocean's surface transfers Energy from wind to Water. Tsunamis are my most terrifying form. Generated by underwater Earthquake, these monster waves wreak destruction when they make landfall.

■ Omnivore

My name means "all eater"—I consume both plants and animals. I come in all shapes and sizes, and my teeth are built to slice flesh, but also to crunch up plants.

▷ Ocean

I am the blue-eyed giant, reaching far and wide across Earth's surface. Gaze into my depths and you'll see wonders and mysteries that will blow your mind! My great volume acts as a sink for Sun's energy. I soak up its rays, helping keep Earth warm and affecting Climate. My currents drive the globe's wind patterns.

Although I have just one body, I am subdivided into five. The biggest is Pacific, which stretches majestically between the Americas, Asia, and Australia. Atlantic Ocean—the saltiest—reaches from Europe to the Americas. Warm Indian Ocean hugs the east coast of Africa up to India, while frigid Southern Ocean wraps around Antarctica. Lastly, small, frozen-over Arctic Ocean sits all ashiver at the North Pole. Brrr!

▷ Oort Cloud

I'm a spherical cloud of comets around the edge of Solar System. Darker than coal and colder than a freezer, I have never been directly observed. My dirty balls of rock and ice have a split

personality—they're quiet and unassuming in the far-flung regions of space, but once past Jupiter and warmed by Sun, they grow tails of water and Carbon Dioxide's vapors.

■ Optics

Look here, I'm the science of the way Light behaves, and I set my sights on Reflection, Refraction, and Diffraction.

▷ Orbit

A whirling dervish, I'm the path an object follows around Planet, Sun, or Star when forward Motion balances out Gravity's pull. If an object traveled any faster, it would shoot off into

space; any slower and it would crash to the ground. With me, the object curves around Planet and back to where it started.

■ Orbital

Not quite an Orbit, more of a fluffy, blurred idea of one, I am the zone around the edge of Atom where Electron lurks. No one can say exactly where, but it's in me somewhere.

▽ Orbiter

I take a one-way trip to space. Once I've gone up, I'm not built to come down again in one piece. I'm a spacecraft with the job to go into Orbit around Planet or a moon. As Satellite, I am a common orbiter of Earth, but I also go further in the name of exploration. I've been sent to all planets except Mercury, Uranus, and Neptune, and hang around for years. My orbital path normally sends me spiraling over every part of my new home's surface, so I can send back detailed data.

■ Ore

I am not a useless chunk of Rock, I am a valuable er . . . chunk of Rock. I contain compounds of Metal, and miners dig me up for purifying. Normally I am a Carbonate, Oxide, or Sulfate.

Organs

We are the fleshy factories, metabolic multiplexes that the body needs to survive. We are vital for vitality. Beneath our sinew and slime, we are built from Tissue, each one working on its own task. We work alone, but are supported by a squad of squishy supporters to make up a body system. Each one runs one fundamental function: breathing, digestion, waste removal, transportation, defense, or communication.

Brain

Skin

Spleen

Pancreas

Bladder

Heart

Lungs

Kidneys

Liver

Stomach

■ Organelle

My name sounds like "little organ," doesn't it, and that kind of sums me up. I'm the machinery inside Cell that does all the hard work. I come in several forms: Chloroplast, Mitochondrion, and Endoplasmic Reticulum are all versions of me. Biologists figure I am the result of simple Bacterium and Archaea ganging together inside single protective Membrane. The result is the complex form of Cell we see today—inside your body and across the animal and plant kingdoms.

▷ Organic Chemistry

Once upon a time, this group of compounds was thought to be made only by living organisms, so it was given the name "organic." That is not true, but the name stuck. It now means the study of Carbon's compounds. Nine out of ten compounds are organic, including Hydrocarbon, and they form the basis of Life on Earth. So it's important stuff!

■ Organism

Every single thing that is alive can be given this name—from Amoeba and aardvark to slime mold and slit-faced bat.

■ Ornithology

Anything feathered is my friend, because I am the science of birds. Compared with other wildlife, Bird is easy to spot, so amateur ornithology—birdwatching—is a big pastime.

▽ Oscillator

I'm always in Motion, but I never get anywhere. Bouncing or swinging around a central point of stillness, I'm a kind of energy store. Give me a shove to get me going, and I convert Kinetic Energy into Potential Energy and then flip-flop the other way to make movement out of all that potential. Each oscillation—swing, twist, shimmy, or bounce—lasts the same amount of time and moves the same distance. Eventually Friction robs me of Energy—push me again!

■ Osmoregulation

Thirsty? That's me sending a message. Need to use the "water closet"? Yes, please, you're talking my language. I'm the system for controlling Water in the body. Too much or too little, I'll know what to do.

■ Osmosis

I like things equal, so when I find unequal solutions on either side of a semipermeable membrane, I'll act. I push Water through the barrier to even things out. This way I'm a driving force within Cell and Tissue.

▷ Osteoblast

A tough little hard hat, I lay down calcium phosphate to make Skeleton. Collagen goes into the mix, too. This keeps Bone a little flexible and makes it less brittle.

■ Oxide

Name that Compound: it's got Oxygen's ions bonded to Metal or another Cation. Oxide is the name that the chemical godfather Antoine Lavoisier came up with. Water is an oxide (of Hydrogen), and so is rust (formed when Iron reacts with Oxygen in Air.)

▷ Oxygen

Colorless, odorless, and tasteless, I am behind most chemical reactions. Made up of molecules each containing two atoms (O_2), my gas combines readily with other substances in "oxidation reactions" to release Energy. When you breathe me in, I slip into your bloodstream. Once I'm inside your body, Cell uses me to fuel life-sustaining Chemical Reaction.

▽ Ozone

Made up of three oxygen atoms joined together, I am light blue as Gas, dark blue as Liquid, and a deep violet-black as Solid.

At ground level, I'm a real nuisance. Thanks to Chemical Reaction when powered by sunlight, I form irritating, throat-tickling Smog, polluted with Hydrocarbon and Nitrogen Oxide. I am at least 1,000 times better than Carbon Dioxide at absorbing Infrared's rays emitted by Earth. Even so, I cause less damage, because I don't stay around as long.

High up in the stratosphere, I'm a superhero. Between six to 30 miles (10 to 50 km) up, a thin layer of me protects Earth from the worst of Sun's ultraviolet rays. My unstable Molecule absorbs Energy so your skin doesn't have to.

O

▷ Paper

For centuries people have come to me in search of knowledge. I'm one of the great inventions of ancient China. "Wood" you believe I get made from mashed-up trees? You can use Microscope to see my interlocking cellulose fibers. This stuff builds the woody parts of trees and helps them stay upright.

■ Parallel Circuit

I'm Circuit when made up of interconnected rings of wires, so Voltage is the same in every section (not shared out piecemeal as in Series Circuit). I'm the circuit used most in houses.

▷ Pancreas

Slim and sock-shaped (although without the holes and the smell), I am a factory for Carbohydrate-mulching, Protein-munching, and Fat-guzzling Enzyme. My pancreatic juices contain about 15 powerful chemicals that make quick work of your burger and chips. These are piped through my pancreatic ducts into Intestines.

Besides my digestive work, I have the important task of regulating Blood's sugar levels: too high and Heart and Kidney might suffer; too low and Brain could be starved of fuel. Enter insulin and glucagon, a balancing act of distinction. Insulin tells Liver to store excess sugar in Blood after eating, while glucagon gets Liver to release its stocks when levels are low. Gee, they're my Hormone heroes!

▷ Parasite

I am an unwelcome guest living alongside (or in) some other unfortunate organism (my host), and I hijack its food supplies. I try not to kill my host—I'd be homeless without it, after all—but I don't mind if I trash the place while I am there. I can even change my host's behavior to stack the odds in my favor.

■ Parthenogenesis

Mom can use me to make babies without the help of Dad. Mostly only simple plants and animals can do it. I make Reproduction quick and easy, but all babies are identical.

▷ Particle Accelerator

A real smasher, I pump Pressure onto Matter until it spills Universe's secrets. I'm not talking about Atom here. No, no, no. I'm after the very smallest parts in the mix—so-called Hadron and Quark.

I get my oomph from super-high Energy, which helps me break up nice, stable Atom, which would rather stay whole. From there, it's simple. I use powerful magnets to accelerate the itty-bitty blips to phenomenal speeds and then slam them into one another inside gigantic detectors! Scientists sift through the wreckage to look for evidence of undiscovered new particles. My Large Hadron Collider zaps Particle around a 17 mi. (27 km) circular track, built 328 ft. (100 m) underground. It is colossal equipment for detecting particles smaller than you can imagine!

■ Pendulum

I'm a swish swinger you can count on. No matter how hard you push my hanging weight, I will swing back and forth at a fixed rate. The exact time is set by my length.

▷ Peninsula

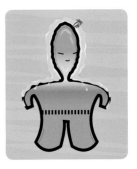

No matter what I do, I always seem to stick out. I never asked to be noticed, but I can't help it. Almost completely surrounded by Water, but never quite cut off, I jut out from Island and Continent. I have to be longer than I am wide. Crucially, I'm well connected and always linked to dry land.

P

127

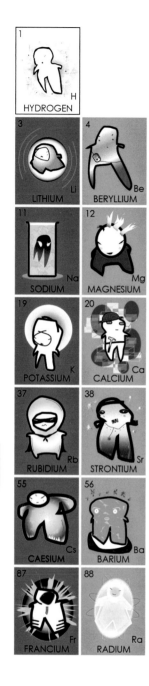

Periodic Table

The Periodic Table was the brainchild of Siberian superchemist Dmitri Mendeleev. In 1869, he arranged the known elements into groups (columns) and periods (rows), leaving gaps in his table for chemical elements still undiscovered at the time. These days the gaps have been filled and there are a total of 118 known elements, but there may be others yet undiscovered. The vertical groups of the table make up "families"—all closely related and liking the same sorts of chemical shenanigans.

P

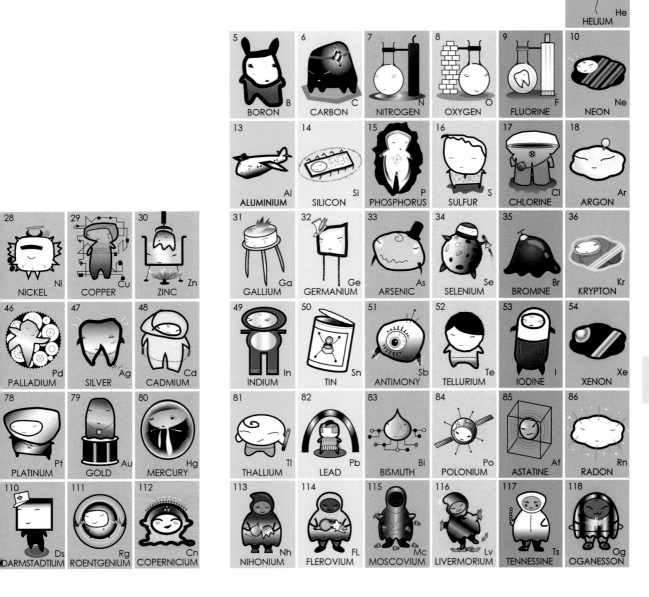

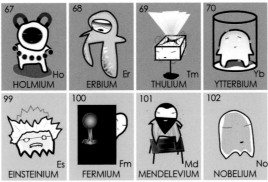

Periodic Table

It's my job to get Element in order. A stickler for organization, I get all 118 elements to line up. Groups (vertical columns) of elements share similar properties. Periods

(horizontal rows) have the same number of electron shells. The metals cluster on the left side and nonmetals on the right.

Peristalsis

I've got rhythm and I use it to send waves through Muscle in Intestines. It's my job to push mushy food (and what comes next) though the gut.

pH

I'm the "pHantom": a secret agent with the code name pH. That's right, small p, big H. I infiltrate Solution to probe it for acidic activity. I then assign Solution a number, from 0 to 14. The more H+ ions drifting around, the more acidic Solution is and the lower my number.

Calm and unbiased, pH 7 sits in the neutral zone. Above this, Solution is completely basic! "pHenomenally" important in your body's tricky chemical environment, my pH has to be just right for a staggering number of complex reactions to happen "pHlawlessly." When you exercise, Blood gets ever so slightly more acidic from carbon dioxide released by Cell breaking down Carbohydrate and Fat for Energy—but too much Acid in Blood causes a total shutdown of all your vital body systems!

Pharming

I'm the *pharmer* of the *phuture*. My plants and animals are genetically modified so that their recombinant DNA produces pharmaceutical drugs.

Using cutting-edge, gene-splicing biotechnology, I get plants and animals to produce therapeutic drugs. Until recently, I used mainly microbes, such as the bacterium *E. coli* and yeast, to make my recombinant proteins in large bioreactors. These days my "drugs factories" might be goats, sheep, and cows producing Protein in their milk or Blood. Taking my medicine is as easy as drinking milk or crunching into a carrot.

Phenotype

A front man, I am the public face of Genotype's hidden hard work. Gene combines with environmental factors to make me—any kind of characteristic (like Eye's color) that can be measured.

Pheromone

A sniff signal, I'm a chemical sent into Water or Air to send a message to other members of Species. Used mostly by Insect and Crustacean, my main job is to attract mates with my irresistible aroma.

Phloem

Sugar is my business. I'm the network of elongated cells that carry Water sweetened with Sucrose from Leaf, where the sugar fuel is made for the rest of the plant.

▷ Phosphorus

I'm a Jekyll & Hyde element—essential to Life, yet wickedly dangerous—a chameleon who appears in black, red, violet, or white. I'm part of DNA's molecule and the energy-carrying molecules used in Cell. Another important use is in Fertilizer. When pure, I catch alight in Air and even burn underwater!

Photochemistry

Chemical Reaction normally likes Heat to be added before it gets going, but in my case it is a blast of Light that delivers Energy.

▽ Photon

I am Universe's fastest thing. With no mass, I whiz along with Speed of Light. I bamboozle physicists with my ability to act like Particle one second and Wave the next. With Electromagnetic Force on board, I speed between Sun and Earth in continuous streams, bouncing off mirrors so that you can see Reflection. I bring Light to the world, but Eye needs to collect about one hundred of me to see anything.

Photosynthesis

My name means "making with light." I use Chlorophyll's green powers to channel sunlight's energy to glucose factories inside Leaf. I work in two stages: a "light reaction" traps Energy, and a "dark reaction" turns Carbon Dioxide and Water into glucose.

P

▷ Physics

I am a science that is all about knowing—or trying to discover—what makes Universe tick. I came about when some naturally nosy people wanted to know why the things around them did what they did. Nothing has changed today, but over the past few centuries, scientists have realized that there are whole worlds both bigger and smaller than our human senses can detect.

■ Piezoelectric

Electricity gives me the shivers. I make crystals such as Quartz vibrate when electrified with Alternating Current. Clocks use vibrating Crystal to count out the time with great precision. I work the other way, too—squeezed Crystal releases electric Charge.

▷ Pipette

I'm a chemist's best friend. My simplest form looks like an eyedropper with a squeezable rubber bulb. My basic job is always the same: I suck up Liquid from one container and deliver it to another as small squirts or drops. My fanciest model is the piston-driven micropipette, which delivers tiny amounts with great accuracy.

■ Piston

Give me a push. Just a little one. I'm a moving part in an engine built to collect the motion energy of expanding Gas, turning it into an up-and-down action.

■ Placebo

I play tricks with your mind and body . . . or do I? If you want the best of me, I recommend not finding out about me. Doctors know that getting some treatment can be enough to help a patient get better—even if it involves pretend medicine. That's me, a harmless dose of nothing, all dressed up to look like a real drug. I am most effective when a patient does not know whether they are taking me or something stronger. As well as helping cure disease, I am used to test if a new drug actually does something during medical trials.

■ Placenta

I'm used by Mammal to supply Blood and food to babies as they grow inside mothers. I develop at the same time as Embyro.

◼ Planet

My name comes from the ancient Greek for "wandering star." Seen with the naked eye I look like any other twinkling star. However, I go my own way, plotting a course across space that show that I'm orbiting Sun and part of Solar System. Solar System has eight of me, but there are billions of others out there, around distant stars.

▷ Plankton

Green and serene, I belong to an entire world of microscopic plants and animals that float free in Ocean. Some of us are super-tiny plants known as phytoplankton.

Soaking up Sun's rays, we produce half of the world's oxygen. Floating alongside, gorging on the veg, are billions of microscopic animals called zooplankton.

▷ Plant Cell

A versatile allrounder, I am equipped to build all the parts a plant needs. I may be a tiny tot, but I keep myself in shape—usually a solidly built box with stiff cell walls. This allows me to stack together in many different shapes. I can split myself in two, making it easy for plants to grow new parts.

I am crammed with organelles: Chloroplast is chock-full of Chlorophyll for converting Sun's energy; Mitochondrion provides Power; and Nucleus coordinates the activity. But I'm literally a sap—that big sac Vacuole sits at my center, and it's full of juicy sap!

◼ Plasma

I'm Gas that gets so hot Atom sheds Electron. That hothead Sun is a ball of me.

▷ Plastic

I'm a highly refined recipe that uses the raw ingredients of Crude Oil. Deep down inside I'm made from long, twisting Polymer, which can be woven and twisted into any shape when hot—and stay that way when cooled. I'm your bag, and also your bottle, your lunchbox, your socks. Plastic is fantastic, but once trashed, I cause Pollution that hangs around for centuries.

P

■ Planets

These characters orbit Sun. Each of the four inner planets has a metal core and a rocky exterior. From Mercury to Mars, they used to be hot stuff, but some of the once-hot liquid centers have now cooled and are solid. Only on Earth will you see Volcano burping out molten Gas and Rock, though there might be volcanoes on Venus or Mars.

The four outer planets, made mostly of gas and ice, comprise—along with their moons—more than 99 percent of the mass of everything that orbits Sun. Powerful atmospheric Force keeps this gang of ring-wearing buccaneers buzzing. On Jupiter, pressure created by layered clouds crushes the gas until it forms seas of liquid buried deep in the haze.

P

Halley's Comet

Mars

Asteroid Belt

Venus

Sun

Earth

Mercury

Pluto

Neptune

Saturn

Meteoroid

Uranus

Jupiter

Plate Tectonics

Hey, I'm cracking up under Pressure as I try to let things slide—and sink and rise. Crust is broken into plates that are constantly on the move, pushing against one another. Normally they go very slowly, but occasionally they give a big jerk, which ends up as Earthquake. Sorry!

Plateau

I'm a lofty plain; a flat area that is high above sea level.

Platinum

The last word in good taste and rarer than Gold, I am a bright, shiny Metal found in southern Africa and Russia. My name is Spanish for "little silver," but I've outgrown my silvery cousin. I never lose my shine because I'm completely resistant to Corrosion. One of my most valuable uses, like so many of my fellow transition metals, is as Catalyst, getting things going in industrial reactions. You'll find me in the catalytic converter, scrubbing poisons from a car's exhaust.

▷ Pluto

After being thrown out of Planet's club in 2006, I was demoted to mere Dwarf Planet. I orbit Sun face-to-face with my twin, Charon (say "Karon"). Out here, Sun looks like a pinhead, and only a smidgen of its life-giving warmth reaches my frozen world. Sometimes Charon and I nip inside Neptune's orbit and get closer to Sun for 20 years at a time. In 2015, New Horizons swung by to check me out. I showed off my best side, a vast heart-shaped ice field, which was named Tombaugh Regio, after my discoverer.

▷ Plutonium

I was named after Pluto, which was discovered a few years before me. Made by nuclear scientists, a lump of me radiates Heat because I release a lot of radioactive Alpha Particle. In August 1945, a nuclear bomb made from my "239" isotope was dropped on Nagasaki in Japan. It killed or injured close to 200,000 people.

Pneumatic

Huff, puff, huff, puff. I'm a gasbag, full of Air. I'm any device—brakes or a pump, perhaps—that is powered by compressed Gas.

P

■ Poikilotherm

I'm a kind of Ectotherm, but I try to keep my body's temperature stable by basking in sunshine or burrowing into cool ground.

▷ Pollen

Tough and intrepid, I'm all man. My mission is to find the female parts of plants of my species and fertilize them to make Seed. But I get up the noses of some people and even make them cry.

Let me set the record straight. One way of getting around, if you are microscopically small like me, is to be blown about by Air. S'not funny for hay fever sufferers! Insect visiting Flower for nectar gets me stuck to its legs and I end up on the gooey tip of a pistil. Then my coat cracks open and I drill into the ovary to help make Seed. My outer coat is so tough that I last for thousands of years.

▷ Polygon

All hail the queen of the 2-D flatlands! All shapes made with straight lines is one of me. I can be regular or irregular, and it doesn't take long to spot the difference. Irregular, and I'm a jumble with sides of different lengths and crazy angles. Regular, though, and there's a little more finesse: my sides are all the same length, and my angles are all the same, too.

▽ Polyhedron

We're space cadets. We add depth (the third dimension) to Polygon's length and width to make 3-D shapes.

▷ Polymer

I'm possible because millions of simple hydrocarbon molecules (these are monomers) connect to make a giant chain. I can occur naturally—think DNA, Starch, and Protein.

I also occur as man-made types, such as Plastic, which can be anything you want it to be. For a 1970s vibe, just check out polyester —it's like one long polymer daisy chain!

P

◼ Polysaccharide

I am a carbohydrate polymer where Monosaccharide links together to form sugary Polymer. The two big names are Starch and cellulose. Starch is a chain of glucose, which makes a plump and fluffy foodstuff relied on by all of us. Cellulose is also made from glucose, but connected in a twisted fashion. That makes it tough stuff—too chewy to digest. We call it fiber.

▽ Population

How many? That is what I'm always asking. I'm the head count for a group of animals in a city, in a country, or in the world. The human population is growing as people keep on having babies. And with improved health care, we all live longer. All of this means that, year on year, I keep going up.

◼ Positron

Keep me away from Electron. I have the same size and mass but with a positive charge. If we meet, we'll obliterate each other. Antimatter will explain all.

▷ Potassium

I am soft and react with Air, so storing me under oil is essential. This keeps me isolated from contact with Air or Water—if I meet Water, I burn with a lilac flame. Everyone knows that I can be found in bananas, and I am key to many body processes, such as sending signals in nerves and Muscle.

▷ Potential Energy

I'm poised, ready for action and raring to go. I am Energy when stored in a stretched catapult, a coiled spring, a rollercoaster at the top of Ramp, a fully charged battery and . . . a chocolate bar. Having literally loads of potential, I am stored energy that can be converted to other forms.

◼ Power

You may say how much and when, and I'll say Watt. I measure how much energy is used every second. One watt (1 W) is one joule per second.

P

▷ Precipitate

I occur when insoluble Compound forms in liquid Mixture. For example, when Solid won't dissolve in Liquid, it falls to the bottom under Gravity and settles on its own. Or it can be filtered out

or even spun out of Solution in a centrifuge—that's a dizzying option! I am used in some paint pigments. Potassium iodide added to lead nitrate results in a beautiful bright yellow lead iodide, but it isn't used anymore.

▷ Precipitation

Get your umbrella out! Run for cover! I have four teams, each with its own unique outfit. There is common rain that drops in its silky suit; hardnut Hail that plummets and peppers; slow snow

that flakes and drifts; and sneezy sleet that mixes rain and snow in a dribble-drabble mess. Fog, mist, and haze don't fall, so they have nothing to do with me, but if I just stay as water vapor and get Atmosphere steamy, I'm called Humidity.

◼ Predator

Live to eat, eat to live. With that I have to agree. However, I live to kill as well. I am a hunter that eats food fresh, killed with my own fair hands, feet, teeth, claws, beak, or venom. You'll find my kind in all areas of the animal kingdom.

▽ Pressure

Time for a most pressing matter—me! I come about when two things are up against each other. Instead of bouncing apart, one of them just keeps pushing on the other—like tarmac against Wheel on a road. I step in when Force concentrates in a particular area. And the greater Force is, the bigger and more powerful I get, too.

I work with all kinds—just ask Wedge how useful that can be. And I'm all around you as Air Pressure. You'd feel really weird if I left (actually, you'd die!). Your body is built to live and work perfectly well with me giving it a little squeeze. If you really want to feel me, though, go to deep Ocean. All that water above you creates a squishing force. You'll need to be inside a submarine, or I'll really get to you . . . Urgh, too late!

P

139

Primary Producer

I am a plant, Bacterium, or member of the Alga family that uses Photosynthesis to produce glucose and pump out Oxygen. Food Web always starts with me. I make food possible by taking Carbon Dioxide from Air and putting it on the menu, in the form of tasty green veggies. Eat me, I'm good for you!

Product

I am what it says on the box. I am what is produced from raw ingredients, such as reactants in a Chemical Reaction.

Projectile

Best to stand out of my way. I'm a missile, a cannonball, a bullet, and I'll go up and away but then come back down again. The science of Mechanics developed to figure out where I'm going to land. I follow a curved path from launch to impact, a shape called a parabola. The size of the parabola depends on Force, Angle, and Mass.

▷ Protein

I make your body tick, marshalling Chemical Reaction in Cell, speeding up reactions (as Enzyme), making Muscle contract, and allowing DNA to replicate. My long polymer molecules are made of very specific sequences of 20 types of Amino Acid, which fold differently according to their order. Where to find instructions for making every one of me? Better ask Gene.

▽ Protist

I am the ancient one. Billions of years ago, different versions of me evolved into the first plants, animals, and fungi. But mostly I like to be alone. I use much of the same equipment as Cell and Plant Cell (Mitochondrion and Ribosome, for example), but all I need to survive is single Cell. I know what you're thinking, but please don't confuse me with Bacterium!

My pals and I go by many names: Amoeba, Alga, or protozoan. Some of us live like plants, using sunlight to make food; others are hunters that chase prey through the slime before spearing it with a barbed dart. Some of us even do both! We move in mysterious ways, too—propelled by a corkscrew tail, wafted along by hairlike Cilia, or simply by folding our bodies in one direction.

P

▷ Proton

A big, chunky hunk of positivity, I hang out in Nucleus, the center of Atom. I'm a big fellow, about 2,000 times more massive than Electron and just as many times less crazy. You won't

see *me* shooting all over the place making and breaking alliances. I am much more responsible—I'm what gives Atom its identity with Atomic Number.

■ Psychology

There is a hidden world, a world of imagination and thoughts that exists inside Brain. It's my job to investigate this amazing place, but there are many problems to solve along the way. What goes on in one person's head is hard to check against the contents of another person's head. Is the human mind smart enough to figure out its own workings?

▷ Pulley

I have a fantastic rope trick that'll turn your puny pulls into mighty lifts. I start out simple: a rope running over Wheel. Pull down on the rope, and Weight, tied to the other end, goes up. Running the

rope around two wheels means that for every distance you pull down, the other side rises just half as much, but lifts with twice as much force as you pull down with Weight.

■ Pupa

Yawn, I think I'll be a new animal after a deep sleep. I'm the phase in many an Insect's life where the food-obsessed larva transforms into the adult form (Caterpillar becoming a butterfly), which is focused on breeding.

▽ Pythagoras (c. 570–495 BCE)

This ancient Greek mathematician loved to give Brain a good workout. Geometry kept his mind in shape! Pythagoras found out amazing stuff about numbers and shapes —most famously, his theorem on triangles. It was Pythagoras that understood that, although math is counting and business and real-world things, it also exists in a world of its own. This means that you can share ideas with anyone, no matter what language they speak. Even aliens!

P

Q

R

▷ Quark

I belong to a gang of six particles. Along with Electron and Neutrino, I am one of Matter's building blocks but exist at an even deeper level. Invisible to Light, I hide away inside Proton and Neutron in Atom's nucleus. I come in six different "flavors" called Up, Down, Top, Bottom, Strange, and Charm.

I have an electric charge that is either minus one-third or plus two-thirds, so I hang out in groups to get the charge to add up to a whole number. My flavor relates to my taste for mixing with other quarks. Up and Down are the most common and most stable.

■ Quantum

I'm a neat little package of energy that comes in a selection of fixed sizes. There are no half measures with me. You either get all of me or nothing at all. I'm important in Subatomic's world, where things happen differently from where you live, because Energy is "quantized" and comes in set dollops, which keeps everything stable.

▷ Quartz

Extremely durable, I make up a big part of granite. Worn down, my grains make sand. Eventually they help form new rock, such as sandstone.

▷ Quantum Physics

In my strange realm things wink in and out of existence; solid Particle suddenly turns into waves of Energy; and stuff only appears when measured.

■ Quasar

I am blindingly bright, but I am so far away across Galaxy that I appear as a faint red Star to Earth's astronomers. Some say that I am a supermassive Black Hole with super-strong Gravity pulling Gas toward me. As Gas falls toward me and decelerates, it loses Energy as huge flares of Light and other forms of radiation.

▷ Radar

I scan the sky with pulses of radio waves, which bounce off objects, pinging a signal back toward Antenna. This shows the location, direction, and speed

■ Radiation

I get confused a lot. What am I and what not? I am produced by Radioactivity —and can be dangerous; it's best to be honest about that—but I also mean Electromagnetic Radiation. These waves include Radio Wave, Heat, and Light—all of which are mostly harmless.

■ Radiation Sickness

Although Radiation is not all bad, the most energetic types—such as X-Ray and Gamma Ray—can cause all kinds of damage to DNA and Organelle if they get into Cell. Radioactivity's powerful particles are even more of a problem. Exposure to all these bad dudes will kill Cell, especially Skin and Stomach's lining.

▷ Radio Wave

I am the workhorse of the airwaves. Made by whipping Electron up into a frenzy in a thin wire, I am bounced around the world carrying TV and radio transmissions, wireless Internet, and all your phone calls and texts. I can travel out across space, so astronomers go gaga for me. Radio telescopes listen in to the pops and crackles of invisible galaxies, and search for signs of Life in Universe.

■ Radioactive Dating

When stuff forms, it is made with tiny amounts of radioactive elements. Those elements decay away steadily, and so I can tell you how old something is by counting up what's left. Potassium is good for dating Rock, while radioactive Carbon dates things that were once alive, like Fossil, wood, and cloth.

■ Radioactive Decay

There is more than one way to cut a cake, and more than one way to break up, or decay, unstable Atom. When Proton and Neutron start feeling uncomfortable, excess particles are pinged out. That makes Nucleus smaller and more stable (perhaps). Crushing instability inside Nucleus can also convert Proton into Neutron and back again, changing the way Atom is structured.

Q

R

143

▷ **Radioactivity**

The outcome of a battle between Electromagnetism and Strong Force, I cause Nucleus to spit out Alpha and Beta Particle, and Gamma Ray.

I am used in nuclear power plants, and I also sterilize food and kill cancer cells. My level of activity is measured by Half-life—the length of time it takes me to break down half of the atoms.

■ **Radioisotope**

I'm an unruly kind of Isotope. My unusual Nucleus turns me into a radioactive rogue.

■ **Radius**

Circle around to get the measure of me. I am the central figure of a circle—the distance from its center to its perimeter. Just double me to make a diameter.

▷ **Radon**

Like my other "noble" family members, I'm almost immune to Chemical Reaction, whereas Radioactivity gives me a sparky character. I can give people lung cancer because I give off harmful radioactive Alpha Particle. And because I am so heavy, I can build up in basements.

▽ **Rainbow**

Mine is a multicolored magic that brings a smile to your face. My looping bands of bright color are made by two bittersweet pals of mine—rain and Sun.

Isaac Newton investigated why my lovely colors always appear in the same order, and named it a spectrum. You see, when light enters a drop of rain, it slows down just enough for the different frequencies bundled up inside white light to split. Light bounces off the back of the raindrop and is reflected in all its glory as red, orange, yellow, green, blue, indigo, and violet. Because I'm a purely optical phenomenon, you can chase me, but you'll never find the point at which I touch the ground—the rainbow's end. I'm afraid the same can be said about that pot of gold. It just ain't there!

Q

R

■ Rainforest

A riot of wild colors and wilder creatures, I'm home to more animal and plant species than any other Biome! My nature comes from my tropical temperament. It's constantly warm and wet within my bounds, so trees and plants produce Flower and Fruit at pretty much any time. (I have a "dry season," but it's still very, very wet.)

▷ Ramp

Lifting is hard work. Big, strong Force is needed all at once, and it can be just too much. Push the load up my slope instead. I break Work up into many smaller steps.

■ Rare Earth Element

Despite my name, I belong to a squad of heavy metals that are not all that rare in Rock and Mineral. I am tricky to separate and purify, though, which is why my discovery came later than that of other natural elements. I have amazing uses in magnets and Optics—the dude that makes the essential ingredients in digital tech.

■ Ratio

You've got five marbles in your hand, right? Two are red, three are blue. The ratio of red marbles to blue ones is two to three—that's 2:3. You can also use me for the odds (or chances) of something happening. If you toss a coin, there are two possible results, both equally likely: heads or tails. The odds of getting heads or tails are 1:1.

■ Reactant

I am the raw material used by Chemical Reaction. Mix more than one of me with Energy, and I transform into Product.

▽ Reactivity Series

I'm an explosive idea and the secret behind Chemical Reaction! I'm a chart that tells you who will win in a head-to-head chemical competition. The more reactive Metal is, the more readily it will lose Electron to form positive Ion. Metals high up on my series are more likely to combine with Oxygen to tarnish their shiny surfaces. Wanna know the secret? The most reactive metal is cesium, then rubidium, Potassium, sodium, lithium, Calcium, and Magnesium. At the unreactive end are Lead, Copper, Silver, Gold, and, finally, easygoing Platinum.

Q

R

145

▷ **Red Blood Cell**

Forever young, I'm a specialist trained to bring life-giving Oxygen to Cell. My doughnut shape means just one of me can carry a billion of Oxygen's molecules.

▷ **Red Dwarf**

I'm small and always cool (for a star) but have strength in numbers. As Galaxy's most common star, I'm never heavier than Sun and shine only faintly.

▷ **Red Giant**

Call a doctor! I'm swelling up and Temperature is low! I've gotten much colder, I'm embarrassed to say, and have turned red. I was not always like this. For ten billion years, I was a full-powered dwarf star. Life was simpler then, when I was burning Hydrogen, converting it into Helium.

When Hydrogen ran low, I started burning it outside Core, huffing and puffing to make enough Pressure to keep on going. Once Hydrogen's supply was gone, I thought I'd use Helium instead, and I've begun fusing its atoms into larger ones such as Carbon and Oxygen. It's hard work, and I've had to grow much bigger to do it. In me, Energy is now spread thinly, giving me this cooler look. I'm running out of time and my strength and will eventually fade away.

▷ **Red Shift**

Star's color can tell you how large and how hot it is. My job is to reveal its motion, too. I do that by stretching Light. You see, doing so makes Wavelength grow longer, and it is this that turns the color redder. Astronomers use me to show that Universe is getting bigger.

■ **Reflection**

I let Light bounce off things. Without my action, everything would look black and lightless. If my reflected beams are kept in order, I'll make a mirror image of you. Here's looking at you, kid.

Q

R

■ Refraction

Stand by for course correction. Light's beams always move in straight lines, but I can shift their direction as they shine into and out of see-through materials like Glass and Water. The swerve is caused by shifts in Speed. (Light moves slower in Water compared to Air, for example.) My beam bending has many effects. Underwater objects are not where they seem, and Lens uses me to focus Light.

■ Relative Speed

Speed is measured from a point at a stand still, but I am the great comparer, so I measure how fast one object moves in relation to another on-the-move item. High-speed objects that move in the same direction may have only slow Relative Speed, but if they go head to head, I'll give Speed an enormous boost.

■ Relativity

More than 100 years old, I'm still the brightest theory in astronomy and big-picture Physics. I came out of Albert Einstein's brain when he tried to understand why Speed of Light is always constant—no matter the relative speed of Light's source and the observer. To make that work, time and space could not be fixed. Instead they change relative to each other as Energy moves through them. It gets pretty weird, but my theory passes new tests time after time.

■ REM

Your eyes move beneath heavy lids, and I stand for Rapid Eye Movement. I'm the phase of sleep when you are dreaming.

▽ Renewable Energy

I'm a ray of hope for a world choking on fumes from burning Fossil Fuel. I harness Energy from sources that are always available. Solar Power uses panels to collect Sun's energy and to heat Water in pipes. Photocells can directly convert Sun's rays into Electricity. Geothermal power uses the heat under our feet to make steam for driving Turbine. Wind turbines use the power of blustery days to whirl propellers around to generate Electricity, while Hydroelectricity—the number one renewable—uses running or falling Water to do the same.

■ Reproduction

Copy cat! Every organism can reproduce to create a close, but not identical, version of itself.

Q

R

▽ Reptile

I am most likely to be found lying out in the sunshine. There's nothing I love better than soaking up some rays. I am not at my best in the morning—my cold blood means that I am a sluggish starter, and I have to wait to warm up before I can get down to a day's business. But I can afford to lie around—I only need to eat about one-fifth as much as warm-bloodied Mammal and Bird to keep my body in good working order.

I might look lazy, but don't be fooled: I have a long history. Way back, my Dinosaur cousins ruled the world. Perhaps my glory days are gone—but some of my kind are still at the top of their game: you'll know what I mean if you ever come eye-to-eye with a grinning crocodile or meet a death-dealing cobra with syringe-like fangs.

■ Resistance

You shall not pass! No Electric Current here. Okay, some of you have pushed through, but the rest of you stop now. No further! All right I'll let that bunch get by . . . but I'll keep on resisting Current's flow. I put up a fight against Electricity, and waste its Energy by converting it to Heat. Superconductor has found a way to get rid of me completely.

■ Respiration

I'm the name for the chemical process in Mitochondrion that releases Energy from glucose, so keeping Organism alive.

▷ Ribosome

I am the craftsman that builds Protein. I read the recipe for each one from DNA's ancient code. The code arrives by messenger RNA. My delicate workshop assembles each

Amino Acid one by one in the order set out by Gene. You will know about many of my products already: Muscle, Enzyme, and Hormone, for example.

▷ River

My life starts out up high. Fed by rainfall, I trickle downward to the valley floor, swelling as smaller streams join in. I meander on until I spill into Lake or Ocean.

■ RNA

I live in the shadow of my dazzling cousin, DNA. And I'm the one who does all the work! Like a spy selling secrets, I make a copy of DNA's genetic manual and spread it through Cell. I unravel DNA's double helix into two strands and then mold my body to fit with one of them. Then, with the help of Ribosome, I follow the instructions to make Protein for the body's workers.

▽ Robot

At your service, I'm a mechanical slave built to work, no questions asked. I started as a factory worker, with Microchip for a brain and hydraulics powering my mega-strong arm. Today, my best designs copy the bodies of animals: fishbots, dogbots, wormbots, even jellyfish droids.

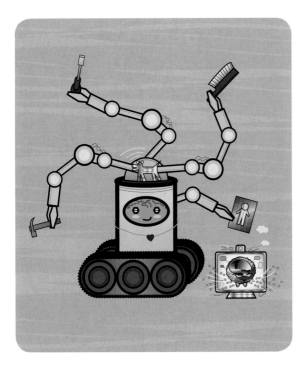

▷ Rock

I am the stuff that forms a crusty scab on Earth's surface. You can thank me for keeping your feet on solid ground. Look closely and you'll see that I am made up of little grains. Surface rock is slowly eroded by Water, wind, and Weather. I get ground down to dust, although new Rock is made all the time.

▷ Rocket

5 . . . 4 . . . 3 . . . 2 . . . 1 . . . Lift off! Hold on to your hat as I blast you through Earth's atmosphere and into outer space. I'm a reaction engine that operates by throwing Mass at high speed out of my rear to create thrust. In space's Vacuum, there is no Air to burn Fuel, so I carry Oxygen with me.

▷ Root

Shy, retiring, and very down-to-earth, I prefer to bury myself in my work. I take up Water and essential minerals from the soil and provide a solid base for future growth. I also store any spare Starch in swellings, such as potatoes, carrots, and turnips, which humans love (mostly).

Q

R

Salt

I am best known as common salt, the white grains used in food. However, in chemistry I am any compound made by Acid.

Saltpeter

Modern chemists call me potassium nitrate, but my other name is much older. I am the third ingredient in gunpowder, after charcoal and Sulfur. I've also got a long history as Fertilizer. I used to be dug up in salty Desert, but now I am made in factories.

Satellite

Peer up into the night sky sometime and you might see me. I look just like Star, but gaze for long enough and you'll see that I am on the move, silently circling Earth.

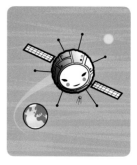

Orbiting overhead, some versions of me monitor Planet's Weather and surface conditions, while others carry telephone calls and TV signals. Some operate a Global Positioning System (GPS), to tell you where you are. We make great spies, too, so be good now. Most of us hang out in low Earth orbit (LEO), and life ends in a blaze of glory when we burn up in Earth's atmosphere.

Saturated Fat

I'm made from complex carboxylic acids that use up all their bonds to hold Hydrogen's atoms. It makes me solid and lumpy. Animal fat is more likely to be saturated than the oily fats in plants, which are unsaturated.

Saline

I'm a solution of Salt and Water. In nature I trickle through Rock, leaving deposits of Crystal. Doctors make their own supply of me for cleaning and hydrating a sickened body.

Saliva

I'm the slobbery dude who makes your food slushy and easy to swallow. It's me that helps Tongue taste. I'm packed with Enzyme and get Digestion going before food even reaches Stomach. Those squidgy Glands pump me out—there are two under Tongue, two beneath the jaw, and two under Ear.

▽ Saturn

Forget about the charms of lovely Venus: I am Solar System's true pearl. I grace the skies dressed in creams and browns, with bands around my middle and a six-sided crown of clouds floating over my north pole. Electric blue lights play around both my poles, a lot like Earth's northern and southern lights.

Like a skilled Hula-Hoop dancer, I spin rings around my middle. Made up of everything from dust to car-size boulders of ice and rock, these flat rings are kept in place by my moons' Gravity. My dazzling hoops are very thin, about 165 feet (50 m) and can be seen stretching out more than 155,350 miles (250,000 km). I'm made of lightweight Gas—so light that I'd float on Water like a giant inflatable ball (if you could find a big enough tank)!

■ Savanna

A totally tropical Grassland, I'm mostly found in Africa (where I'm also known as veld), but I sprout in Australia, too. I grow where there is not really enough rainfall for lush Woodland or Forest but just enough to stop the land turning to Desert. I often have a few small, slow-growing trees dotted around.

▷ Schrödinger's Cat

Dreamed up by Erwin Schrödinger, I exist in the "quantum" world, where—until observed —Particle can be in two places at once. Erwin imagined me shut in a box with a radioactive source. If the source decays, it releases poison gas from a bottle and I kick the bucket. If not, I stay alive! No one knows when the source decays, so until someone looks in the box, it is neither decayed nor not decayed—so I am both alive and dead!

▷ Screw

Do you catch my thread? That's the name for the spiral that runs from my tip and goes to my head. Look closely and you'll see that I'm a two-in-one Machine team— Ramp twisted around an axle. With each turn of the axle, Ramp pulls on whatever is there. I make a super-strong fastening. Once screwed in, I don't come out easily. Let's twist!

▷ Seaborg, Glenn T. (1912–1999)

This American was the discover of ten elements made in labs in the 1950s. In 1994, seaborgium, a heavy metal, was named after him.

▷ Season

Earth bows a little as it orbits because Axis is on a slight tilt. As a result, the north nods toward hotshot Sun in the summer, and the south faces away (its winter). Six months later the north is tilted away, so it is in the depths of winter (the south is summery now). The poles notice the biggest extremes, while Equator gets a year-round supply of sunshine.

▷ Seawater

I cover more than two-thirds of Earth's surface and hold 97 percent of its water in Ocean. Every 1 lb. of seawater has about 0.6 oz. of dissolved salts (35 g per 1 kg). While albatrosses can drink me, any thirsty sailor won't be so lucky—fatal concentrations of Salt in Blood cause fits, seizures, and a grisly death.

My salt content makes me different from Fresh Water. Things float more readily in me because of my increased density, which makes it easier to swim in me. I also freeze at around –28°F (–2°C), not 32°F (0°C), so rarely freeze over.

■ Second

Minute is first to my second. Our pal Hour is first divided into 60 minutes, and Minute is then divided into 60 of me.

▷ Sedimentary Rock

Handsome in my honeyed tones, I make up 80 percent of Earth's land area. When Rock is worn away by wind and rain, River carries broken pieces away.

When River lacks the energy to take them farther, the fragments settle as sediment. The layers build, squeezing out Water and turning the sediment into solid Rock—me!

S

▷ Seed

I am the great hope, a tiny parcel that contains everything needed to make a new plant, sent out to colonize Earth.

I'm tough and can survive without food, Water, or Air for hundreds of years. I am scattered in the wind or hitch a ride on animals. Often I get eaten as part of Fruit, and slip through an animal's guts onto the ground.

▷ Seedless Plant

I belong to a bunch of ancient plants. I use Chlorophyll to make food from sunlight. But I don't have anything as pretty as Flower or as tasty as Fruit. Unlike Flowering Plant, I breed using

Sperm and Egg, not Pollen. Instead of Seed, I spread spores, which grow into new plants.

Seaweed likes to live beside the seaside but has to cope with being dried out and soaked through again twice a day! Moss and flat liverworts were the first land plants, about 475 million years ago. Some 175 million years later, tree ferns also covered the land.

■ Seismology

When Earthquake strikes, it's me that studies its Energy's waves as they move through and around Earth. They're "seismic"!

▽ Semiconductor

I'm a technological wizard. I "conduct" affairs in every piece of electronic equipment, telling Electric Current where to go and how to act. The funny thing is, I'm not terribly good at conducting Electricity, but I've made my vice a virtue.

I'm made using metalloid elements, which are strange materials that don't quite know whether they are Metal or Nonmetal. But I can't perform unless I've had some impurities added first. This "doping" adds in or takes away electrons that let Electric Current flow —but only in certain directions, which is key to my fantastic usefulness. Semiconductor "sandwiches" are made into Transistor's switches on Microchip. These can create all kinds of complicated logic decisions and make me the brains of Computer.

S

Senses

Crack open toughnut Skull, that hard headcase of yours, and you'll find a soft type called Brain. Despite being a gooey wobbler looking like a disgusting dessert, this clever dude is the leader of this sparky gang of incredible senses. With the help of nerve cells and the coordinating genius of Brain's lieutenant, Spinal Cord, they have the good sense to tell Brain what's happening inside and outside your body. It's thanks to these guys that the world you live in looks, feels, sounds, smells, and tastes the way it does.

S

Smell

Sight

Hearing

Touch

Taste

Series Circuit

I connect components in a long chain, one after the other. That means Electric Current only has one way to go and the same amount passes through each part of me. I'm no splitter like Parallel Circuit. My set up sees Voltage divided between the components, with each getting a fraction of the total. As the number of components goes up, available Voltage goes down. This makes Electric Current drop as well—so my bulbs dim, speakers fade, and Microchip fails. Parallel Circuit has more oomph than I do but uses Power much faster.

Sexual Reproduction

I mix things up a bit to make babies ready for what the future holds. Female can only make babies that are identical to herself. Involving Male adds in some new DNA to create some variety—the spice of Life.

▷ Silicon

Combined with Boron or Phosphorus, I become Semiconductor. These special powers gave birth to Microchip and the Computer Age.

Silicon Valley in northern California is named after me. I take many different forms. As the second most abundant element in Earth's crust, I crop up in sandstone, Quartz, flint, and most other minerals. As silicone (that's Polymer, when made up of me, Oxygen, and some organic chemicals), I'm in rubber, adhesives, and body implants. In Glass, I'm perfectly clear. In Quartz's watches and clocks, I keep time, while as silica Gel, I keep products moisture-free. You'll find silica Gel in packets in boxes of electrical goods.

▷ Silver

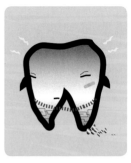

Whether made into money, jewelry or ornaments, I have always been coveted for my shininess. But I always lose out to Gold because I can't help forming a tarnish layer of black silver sulfide when I come into contact with Air. As light-sensitive silver bromide, I was once used to capture old photographs and movies for the "silver screen."

Sinus

I generally mean any hidden space in the body. My main location is up inside Nose, where I form air cavities around Eye.

▷ Skeleton

I'm the body's hardcase that offers protection and support to the surrounding softies. I am the superstructure where the rest of the body parts hang out—without me

you'd be a flop. In me, Bone is stronger than Steel and can carry five times its own weight. I achieve this with a mix of flexible collagen and rock-hard calcium phosphate.

▷ Skin

I am the single most advanced material known to humankind —hardwearing, waterproof, super-stretchy, and very sensitive. I'll also keep you warm or chill you out, and fix myself

when broken. I'm your first line of defense against sticks, stones, and infectious diseases. On my surface, all the cells are dead—you are always carrying about 45 pounds (2 kg) of dead skin—as I renew myself every month.

▷ Skull

I'm a bonehead not a braniac, but I'm still pretty sophisticated. My bony mask holds delicate sense organs. I'm also a super-hard shell that saves soft Brain from knocks.

▽ Smog

I'm a flagon of foul Air, a can of cough and splutter. A thoroughly unpleasant sandwich of the words "smoke" and "fog," I stick in the throat and make life a misery for city dwellers. I turn Air soupy with Pollution, and when I get really nasty, I can burn your throat and eyes.

I exist in a haze of fine, almost invisible particles of soot, dust, and chemicals hanging in Air. In colder months, I'm caused mostly by people burning wood and coal to keep warm. In the summer, Gas from burning Fossil Fuel combines in sunlight with Hydrocarbon to make a "photochemical" cloud, containing two-faced Greenhouse Gas member Ozone. Low-altitude Ozone is no fun. It's a reactive chemical that attacks plants and buildings, not to mention delicate Lung!

S

157

▷ Solar Power

Every hour sunlight delivers more energy to Earth than humans use in one year!

It's my job to get hold of it. It will never run out like Fossil Fuel. I use silicon Semiconductor to make Electric Current from Light or to capture Sun's thermal energy by heating Water. I alone can solve the energy crisis and Climate Change *and* I produce zero Pollution. What are you waiting for?

▷ Solar System

I am one big, happy family living in a region of space a million times wider than Earth. Because Sun holds almost all of the weight, its Gravity makes everything else spin around it. That's eight planets (with 166 known moons), five dwarf planets, billions of asteroids, comets, and meteoroids, and interplanetary dust.

The main planets circle Sun in the same direction, and on a flat disk around Sun's center. Distances between them are immense—Saturn is twice as far from Sun as its inner neighbor, Jupiter.

▦ Solar Wind

Pushed out from Sun's gaseous surface, I work with Light to "blow" gusts of electrified Particle out into space.

▽ Solid

Trustworthy and dependable, I don't go for anything showy or high-energy. I'm built well and am meant to keep my shape. With a high melting point, I definitely don't flow. I'll sit motionless instead, which is handy if you want to make objects out of me or use me to contain playful, slippery Liquid.

With my atoms packed closely together, I resist squeezing and changing volume. My atoms often have Crystal's structure—a regularly repeating pattern—but certain solids, such as Glass, have an amorphous (random) internal structure. Raising my internal energy (using Heat, for example) will eventually turn me into Liquid. Polymer is a solid in which long, flexible Molecule makes it plastic. Protein is a biological solid found in all living matter.

Solution

I'm never odd, and always even—evenly mixed that is. I am Mixture where Solid or Gas (the solute) is mixed into Liquid (the solvent) so completely that you cannot discern where one ingredient begins and the other ends. In other words, it's dissolved.

Solvent

Always Liquid, I am a chemical that is good at dissolving other substances. Water is my ultimate representative because its molecules have charged ends that tease apart Ionic Bond to aid in its mixing.

Sonic Boom

I am the cracking noise left behind when an aircraft flies faster than Sound.

Sound

I surround you—no matter where you go, I'm there, vibrating in your ears. Even the quietest sound moves your eardrum. This is a good thing because it lets you talk with other people and listen to the world's beautiful noises. Kids love lots of me, but older folk tend to like me less and gripe about me more.

I get from place to place by causing small disturbances that are passed along in the same way that shoves and jostles move through a crowd of people. Watch a loudspeaker at work and you'll see how the speaker cone pushes and pulls at Air around it. I travel pretty fast, but supersonic jets can "break the sound barrier," releasing huge amounts of Energy as Sonic Boom. Thunder is a pressure wave that we can hear, made by Lightning's heat.

Space Shuttle

I was the first reusable spacecraft to travel to space. I'm retired now, but for 30 years I lifted people and equipment into low Earth orbit (LEO). I had a space plane called Orbiter with an external fuel tank slung beneath, and two solid rocket boosters (SRBs) to blast me off.

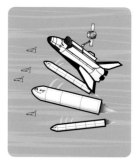

Space Suit

Don't step outside without me! I have as many as 14 layers to offer comfort and safety. My clip-together parts make a pressurized zone inside with Air to breathe among the nothingness.

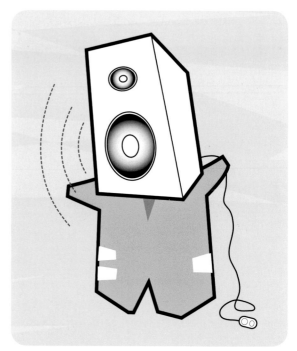

S

159

Space-Time

Welcome to the fourth dimension! I am a higher being all around you—the framework on which Universe is built—yet your puny human senses cannot perceive me. You're used to seeing in only three dimensions, but really space is made of four: height, width, depth . . . and time.

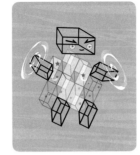

Changing one dimension will alter all the others. Time does not have a steady ticktock. It runs slower for things traveling really fast and also goes into slo-mo near heavy stuff like Black Hole.

Sparticle

I may not be real at all, but one way to solve the mysteries of Quantum Physics and Dark Matter is to pair every subatomic particle with a heavy, but invisible, super particle—or "sparticle" for short. This idea comes from a set of theories called supersymmetry. Do I exist? The person to ask is Particle Accelerator. So far, the guy says no. Shame!

Species

Gather round, I'm a very special group of organisms. I'm made up of animals or plants—or another kind of Life—that share many similarities. However, none of us are truly identical. Our big connection is that we can make babies. Very few outside the group can do that. Biologists are so impressed they give us two names, emphasized with italics. Your human species name is *Homo sapiens*.

Speed

Everybody's in a hurry these days, and that makes me a really hot commodity! Internet connection speed, tight deadlines, and speed dating—I'm where it's at. But what's the rush? Chill.

Although I tell you how quickly you can get from A to B, I'm a balanced type, and I like things to be placed evenly. If an object has no force pushing or pulling it, it will coast along merrily at the same unchanging speed . . . or just stay still! Unlike Acceleration (always in a hurry to change my pace), I am steady. Don't worry, you'll get there in the end. No Force, no sweat! There are loads of ways to measure me. Pilots use Mach Number, which compares a jet's speed to the speed of Sound. Sailors use "knots," a ropey old-school method.

Speed of Light

The top speed in the Universe, you can't see me coming. I'm the speed of Photon and other massless particles. Nothing with mass can go as fast as me. It is a law of Physics.

Sperm

Get set. Go! Lovely Egg and I make new Life. I'm a little guy with a big job. In humans, I start in the testes, a man's sperm factory. I travel upstream towards the penis. If everything goes "swimmingly," I enter Female's body and whip my long tail for the hour's swim to my eggy destination.

Spinal Cord

The king of Speed, I'm a zippy-zappy dude who keeps you on your toes. I'm a slinky, slippery type who runs up the middle of S-shaped Spine. I am your body's information highway and, boy, I've got some nerve!

It's through me that Brain gets wind of what your sense of touch is up to. Nerve signals whiz along my length like mini electric pulses and provide a high-speed link that warns of imminent danger. Quick as a flash, Brain sends an order to move and I jolt your reactions into life. This is how you can hit the brakes on your bike before you hit the wall. But I don't always need Brain to get you out of trouble. Say you're about to dip your fingers into boiling water. Well, it's me, and me alone, who makes you whip them out way before they burn. It's totally electrifying!

Spine

You can thank me when you stand on your own two feet and hold your head up high. Reach around to the middle of your back and you'll find my graceful line. I'm a stack of bony rings. At my very top are the axis and atlas bones that allow you to nod for "yes" and shake for "no." At my very bottom (and yours!) is the coccyx—your tailbone.

Spiracle

I'm an air hole used by Insect and other Invertebrate types. Air wafts through me into the body. You never see a bug out of breath.

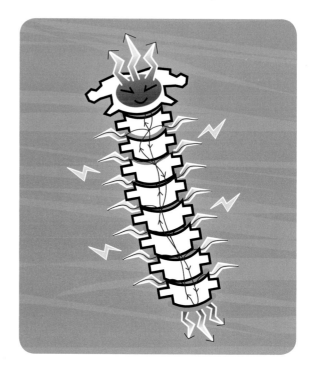

Stamen

I stand and deliver—deliver Pollen, that is. Rising from the depths of Flower, my tall slender frame is tipped with anthers, where Pollen forms and prepares for its life's work. In wind-pollinated plants, I hold my head into the breeze to release my cargo. If Flower relies on Insect or another animal to move Pollen from Flower to Flower, I skulk closer to the nectar, the sugary drink offered to visitors, so they rub against me and pick up a dusting of Pollen's grains as they slurp.

Standard Model

I'm a squad of 17 fundamental particles that are needed to make Universe. Matter is built from the likes of Quark and Electron and comes as 12 particles, known as the fermions. Force is controlled by the five bosons that include Photon and Gluon. The odd man out is the Higgs Boson, which summons Mass for Matter.

▷ Star

I'm a fearsome fireball burning millions, even billions, of ton of Hydrogen every second. I give off Light and Heat using Fusion. More often than not, I'm orbited by scraps of rock and ice better known as Exoplanet.

At the heart of my boiling cauldron, Hydrogen's atoms fuse together to make Helium, releasing enough energy to blow me to smithereens. But Gravity—from my sheer bulk—keeps me together. I have a blast, spraying a stellar wind of charged particles into space. Sun is the star local to you. Be thankful that your planet is protected by a magnetic shield; otherwise, Solar Wind would finish you off!

Starch

Stiff and stodgy when raw, but crispy, crunchy, and yummy when cooked, I'm the main form of Carbohydrate used by plants to store Energy. Seed, Fruit, and Root pack in my complex Polymer to keep a plant alive during cold or dry seasons.

State of Matter

I am something that you can see, touch, feel, or hold—the physical properties of Matter. You'll find four forms of me: Solid, Liquid, Gas, and Plasma. Every Element and Compound can exist in all three states. Most are Solid at everyday temperatures, and many will try to avoid Liquid and go straight to Gas as they heat up. Earth is a wet planet covered in liquid Water, but elsewhere in Universe, Liquid is a strange and rare state.

S

▷ Static Electricity

I may not be as dynamic as Electric Current, but I can move in a flash. As lightning, I kill around 1,000 people a year. I'm caused when insulators rub together. Electron gathers on one Insulator, creating a difference in Electric Charge.

▷ Steel

Mostly made of Iron with a sprinkle of Carbon, I'm tough stuff. I'll bend, but I almost never break and can lift my own weight with ease. I can be rolled and bashed into shape, pulled to make wires, and even melted down so you can start all over again.

▷ Stem

I'm a stiff sort of fellow, a water main for plants. I take Water to Leaf and its friends and deliver food in the form of syrupy sap. In me, Plant Cell is harder than elsewhere, with woody walls that make excellent tubes for slurping up Liquid and keeping a plant upright. Unfortunately, this stiff stuff also makes vegetables stringy.

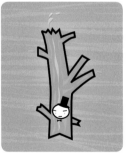

▽ Stem Cell

I am the cell with infinite potential, the Special One, have no doubt! There's no other cell quite like me, because I can become any type of cell I choose. My cellular cousins start and end life as specialists—in Brain or Skin, for example—but me, I'm a mighty morpher.

My unique shapeshifting talents make me incredibly valuable. Just think about it: because I can divide to become anything from kidney cells to muscle or heart cells, I could one day be used to create custom-built organs for transplants. So how do I do it? Well, I multiply, just like Cell does. But when I split, each new Cell gets to choose whether to stay the same or become something different. Mmm, let's see . . . nerve cell? Nah. Muscle cell? Maybe . . .

S

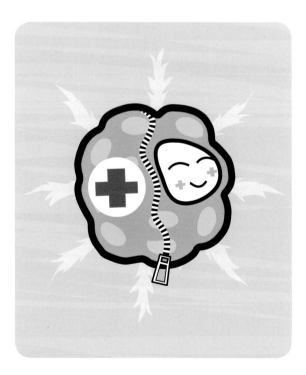

Stoma
I'm a small hole in Leaf that lets Gas in and out. My plural is stomata.

▽ Stomach
Give me some food! I break down food into a nutritious mush called chyme, before passing it on to Intestines. Sure, Tooth, Saliva, and Tongue all do a reasonable job, but I'm a far superior being—a big sloshing, gurgling, glugging vat of Enzyme, Bacterium, and food-dissolving Acid. I've got Muscle, too, mercilessly squeezing and beating your nosh. And if I can't "stomach" something, I give it the old heave-ho with a swift contraction. Enough of your bloated boasting, I hear you say. Okay, okay! After about six hours of my churning, your food begins to look like thick pea soup. My work is done!

String Theory
I can't keep still thinking about why it is that science cannot explain Quantum's world properly. Maybe Electron and Quark are not the smallest things in nature. I reckon instead that all particles are strings that vibrate in all kinds of directions—not just the three everyday directions but several more as well that only exist in tiny spaces. Excited? I am.

▷ Strong Force
At more than 100 times stronger than Electromagnetic Force and ten thousand trillion times tougher than Weak Force, I am Universe's circus strongman.

Inside Atom's nucleus, I do battle with Electromagnetic Force, who makes positively charged protons repel each other violently. I hold it all together. As well as keeping Proton and Neutron tightly imprisoned inside Nucleus, I act on the quarks nested within them, who interact by exchanging my powerful gluon particles. Every time they do so, they change their quantum state, and this keeps 'em attracted to each other.

Subatomic
As my name suggests, I refer to things smaller than Atom. For hundreds of years people thought I was a fantasy. Not possible, they said. Atom means uncuttable, they said, so you can't break it up into something smaller. Well, I showed them. Er . . . I mean no one can see things this small, but my world inside Atom is real. Just ask Electron and Proton.

Sublimation

Liquid is strange stuff. It holds together like Solid but moves around like Gas. If you ask me, its best just to skip over it, and that is what I do. Instead of having a solid melt and then boil when Heat is around, I allow it to jump straight to Gas. Carbon Dioxide is famous for just this. Its cold "dry ice" turns into misty fumes, never wet puddles.

Sulfate

Made by the union of Sulfur and Oxygen, I'm a common mineral class, often snapped up by eager miners as Ore. I'm known for adding color to the grays of drab Rock, with my speciality being deep blue. As calcium sulfate I'm better known as plaster, stucco, and drywall. My main use is for making that nasty fellow sulfuric acid.

▷ Sulfur

Dressed in yellow, I look as harmless as a lemon cupcake. But I have a wicked side as a fun-loving prankster who likes to unleash rotten-egg smells and foul skunky odors.

It's my compounds that stink—hydrogen sulfide is the most likely culprit. I was once known as "brimstone" and featured in fiery descriptions of Hell, because I turn red when melted and ooze from Volcano. Exposed to Oxygen and Heat, I spontaneously combust! These qualities make me an important part of gunpowder. I also cause Acid Rain. I am an essential Element in sulfuric acid—used for making a multitude of other substances.

▷ Sulfur Dioxide

You can't see me because I am a colorless gas, but with a puff of smoke, I make a sharp and suffocating odor (think burned-out matches). A nasty form of Pollution, I play havoc with stuffy Atmosphere. I react with Water to make Acid Rain, and I have a habit of forming choking blankets of Smog.

▽ Sun

Good day! I am the brightest thing in the sky. I dazzle when Earth turns on Axis to face me, and I outshine everything. I have the power to make you smile.

S

▽ Superbug

Full of spite and ready to fight, I'm chortling with glee because I'm turning humans' best defenses against them. I have evolved a resistance to drugs that ward off my invasions, and I'm fast becoming invincible!

Antibiotic might be the wonder drug of modern times, but there's a chink in its armor —when it kills disease-carrying Microbe, it also weeds out the weak. That means less competition for me, which, coupled with my super-resistance, can be fatal. Worse still, Antibiotic can harm colonies of healthy Bacterium that keep me and my super-resistance at bay. What doesn't kill me makes me stronger! My real enemies are good hygiene, handwashing, and, if you're taking antibiotics, making sure you always complete the course.

■ Superconductor

I'm a super-cool material that banishes Resistance completely. I let Electric Current pass without losing Energy.

■ Superfluid

When Temperature is very low, liquid helium loses its resistance to flow, becoming me in the process. I can go anywhere, even up the side of a cup, and am not contained easily!

▷ Supergiant

Live fast, die young, and go out with a bang—that's my motto! I'm one of Universe's monster stars, regularly between 10 and 70 times bigger than Sun.

Supergiants burn thousands of times brighter than Sun. Like a petulant hothead, one day I'll explode in the most terrifying of Universe's cataclysms—Supernova.

▷ Supernova

I am the last thing that happens to Supergiant when it fizzles out of fuel. When this happens, that dude blows its top and I make a bang that shines billions of times

brighter than Sun. I am so fierce that I can outshine Galaxy before fading. After I have ended, you'll find Neutron Star or Black Hole.

S

Surface Tension

Liquid's molecules cling to each other—not as hard as Solid holds on, but enough to keep them together as a blob. That "intermolecular" Force creates me, a force that holds Liquid's surface together. I'll bend and flex, but I don't break right away. I'm also there to stop puddles from spreading indefinitely.

Suspension

I'm a thick sort of fellow, but I'm light at heart. Another kind of mixed-up Mixture, I am lumps of Solid or Liquid that float in Liquid or Gas, like silt in River's water, and as blobs of color pigment in oil to make paint. In me, Solid or Liquid's droplets are small enough to resist Gravity's pull until I'm left to stand perfectly still for a long time. Slowly I'll separate out, sometimes creating sludge and slick.

▷ Symbiosis

Life is so sweet when we just live together, no? Cooperation is the name of the game! You scratch my back and I'll scratch yours.

Bacterium has a bad rap for causing diseases. But some bacteria are helpful. Take gut bacteria, for example. They help you deal with tricky foods like fiber and Lactose, and make meals more digestible. Some gut bacteria even compete against others to knock nasty bugs out of action. And what about the dudes that help plants get a "fix" of Nitrogen from soil? These are good guys! I come in two types. The commensals get the perks but don't return the favor, while the mutualists benefit both partners. Trouble is, my nasty cousin, Parasite, sees things very differently.

Symmetry

Draw a line through a shape so both sides look the same. You've found me.

Synapse

Neuron is a touchy fellow, so it never touches a neighboring Cell. I'm the gap between them, and Neuron sends chemical messengers across to get nerve signals moving.

Synthetic Biology

My game is to make artificial biological systems using a combo of Biology and engineering. In the right hands, I create useful, living devices. No one wants these microbes to turn bad and to overcome the natural defenses of Earth's living things, so some of my designs are never able to reproduce.

S

T

Tachyon

I shouldn't exist and probably don't. I'm a particle that moves faster than Speed of Light. You can't ever see me because I arrive before any light I give out. Once you see me, I'm no longer there.

▷ Taiga

I'm a northern type who dresses in a thick "fir"(tree) coat. Home to some of the world's most inaccessible wildernesses, I contain Earth's most northerly forests and about one-third of all its trees. Where I am, gritty Conifer can last all winter, even with the ground frozen solid.

Taxonomy

Life is for living, sure, with all its variety and diversity, but let's get things organized. I am the science of classifying Organism, and I divide it into taxons (groups). The smallest group is Species, and the biggest is domain. Kingdom, phylum, class, order, family, and genus are all in between. My system shows how Life's forms are related. I used to decide on the groups by Organism's appearance, but today my teams compare DNA and Gene to figure it out.

▷ Technology

Take a look—almost every man-made thing you see is one of my clever inventions! Usually working to solve a problem or make a task easier, I am always looking to the future. I use science to make more useful materials and to design better, more efficient machines.

▷ Telescope

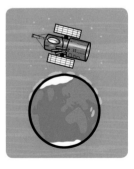

I can see for miles and kilometers—even light years. I use Lens and mirrors to collect distant Light and then magnify it so Eye can see all the details. I'm doubled up to make binoculars for use on Earth, but my biggest versions look far beyond Planet. As well as Light, astronomical telescopes image space using Radio Wave, X-Ray, and every other kind of Radiation.

■ Telomere

Ticktock, I'm a genetic clock. I am a structure found at the ends of Chromosome. Each time Chromosome divides, my tip is destroyed. When I get too short, Chromosome dies.

■ Temperature

Too hot to handle and way too cool for school, I'm a well-known and popular member of the science community. It's my job to reveal how much heat is inside something—Air, Water, your body. I'm measured using Thermometer, and I call on Celsius and Fahrenheit to do all the talking. Serious scientists use Kelvin, which starts at Absolute Zero. My values are not simple; I'm an average figure for Thermal Energy held by the molecules in a substance.

■ Terminal Velocity

Scream if you want to go faster. It won't make any difference. I am the balancing act between Gravity, who makes things fall, and Air Resistance, who is such a drag that gets in the way. You have to fall from a great height to make me appear. At first you'll accelerate down. As you speed up, Friction starts getting involved, creating an opposing force pushing back on Gravity's pull. After about 15 seconds, the two equal out so you stop accelerating. You've hit top speed, or Terminal Velocity. Enjoy the ride!

■ Terrestrial

I'm all about dry land. On Earth, Continent is a terrestrial region surrounded by Ocean. I also mean "related to planet Earth." Mercury, Venus, and Mars are terrestrial planets as well.

■ Tesla, Nikola (1856–1943)

Born in Serbia in 1856, I went to America as a young man and changed the world. I invented the electrical distribution system still used today. It uses Alternating Current and Transformer to get Electric Current on its way.

▽ Tessellation

I just love playing around with shapes, fitting them together so that there are no gaps or overlaps between their edges. I've been around for centuries, making patterns for Islamic tile decorations and Roman mosaics, among other things. I can make regular patterns using equilateral triangles, squares, or hexagons. In a more flamboyant mood, I work with two or more shapes—squares, triangles, or other polygons—to make semiregular patterns.

T

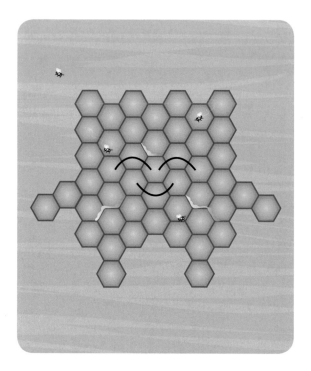

▷ **Test Tube**

Hold me, shake me, and heat me up! Made of Glass, I'm slim, tall, curved at the top, with a round bottom. I'm the playground on which most of Chemistry —organic and inorganic—is played out.
Finger-size, I usually lounge around in racks or am held tightly in the grip of a test-tube holder. I do love to cause a reaction!

■ **Theory**

I'm more than a big idea. I'm a set of explanations for something complicated and important. Scientists use experiments to test me, and that makes me something like truth. Whatever I say is more or less fact— until someone comes up with a better set of ideas to explain it all.

■ **Thermal Energy**
See **Heat**

■ **Thermistor**

A changeable fellow, I'm a mash-up thermal resistor. I'm a component that alters Resistance with Temperature. I'm useful in electric thermometers and temperature-control systems in refrigerators and ovens.

■ **Thermodynamics**

My science describes how Heat moves around. On my watch, Heat always spreads out, heading toward cold, never away.

▽ **Thermometer**

I'm a little piece of magic that you can hold in your hand. Temperature is a very strange concept to pin down. It's something you can only feel. Until Liquid boils, for example, it's very difficult to see how hot or cold it is. Yet I turn that reality on its head and allow you to "see" Temperature and read it off a calibrated (confirmed) scale.

The simplest version of me is a delicate soul in a slender package. I am surrounded by Glass, with Vacuum forming my central column. This makes my liquid independent of Air Pressure. I work on the basis that materials expand and contract as they get hotter and colder. The longer my line, the higher Temperature reads. For accuracy, I am calibrated against known temperatures, such as Water's freezing and boiling points.

T

Thermonuclear

Sorry that I exist. I'm never a good idea. My explosion system uses the power of Fission's reaction to create Fusion's bomb. I make the most powerful bombs ever created—but I was devised never to be used.

Thermoplastic

I'm a common kind of plastic that lives up to that shapeshifting name. Heat me and I go soft as putty. Mold me to your will and I will set as Solid. And then do it all again. In me Polymer is happy to lock into any shape, then detach and strike another pose.

Thermoregulation

I'm Heat's leveler—I keep a body at the right Temperature. I'll fight off hypothermia (too cold) and hyperthermia (too hot) by shivering, sweating, panting, and moving Blood in and out of Skin.

Thermoset

Although I'm Plastic and can be set into any shape when warm, once cooled I become an immovable structure. Adding Heat will not soften me up again. That makes me resilient and useful stuff.

▷ Tide

I'm a bit of a lunatic! As the Moon moves overhead, Ocean's sea level rises and falls. That's me, attracted by Gravity's pull. I'm usually "high" and "low" twice a day.

Time

What am I? Well, everyone knows of me, but no one really knows what I actually am. Where do I come from? Am I real, or did you just create me to make sense of the way Energy keeps moving around in space? Whatever I am, I always go in the same direction—and can never run backward.

▽ Tin

I am too soft for my own good, that's my problem. I melt at a low temperature (for a metal), and below 55°F (13°C), I change from bendable, flexible Solid into a crumbly powder. I get mixed with other metals to make Alloy and that keeps me in shape. (I'm only a thin coating on "tin" cans—they're actually made of Aluminum or Steel.) Mingled with Copper, I make bronze.

T

▽ Tissue

I am the fabulously sloppy stuff that holds you together. When it comes to building your body, humdrum Cell may start the job, but it's definitely me who finishes it. Honestly, Cell would be nothing on its own!

I am the innard wizard! Call me smug, but I can't help it. I ooze class, as I arrange Cell into different groups and layers to make all your gorgeously gloopy insides. Gristle, sinew, marrow, Muscle, Fat, and slippery Membrane—these are all down to me and my meticulous organization.

Even those self-satisfied, puffed-up, complex Organs like Heart, Kidney, Lung, and Skin are made simply by combining layers of my various, wonderfully unctuous functional units. Now that's what I call "organ"-ized!

▷ Titanium

I am gleaming, extremely hard, and very resistant to any type of chemical attack. As a brilliant-white dioxide Compound (me plus two Oxygen atoms), I make excellent paint.

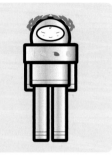

My main use is for superhard Alloy, whose unrivalled combo of lightness and strength means that it often gets used in airplane and spacecraft manufacturing.

■ Titration

I'm a real drip. Scientists use me to add Reactant bit by bit as a way of counting up how many moles are in Solution.

▷ Tongue

A man of taste, I tell Brain what's yummy or yucky when you eat. My surface is covered with lumps, called taste buds. These little guys detect sweet, sour, salty, bitter, and umami (a savory

meatiness) in your food. But, hey, there's more. Thanks to my muscular make up, I can slurp food around your mouth and let you talk a mile a minute. There's no stopping me!

■ Tonsil

One of a pair, I'm a ring of lymphatic tissue guarding the throat. I collect incoming germs and pass on information to Immune System.

T

▽ Tooth

With help from the body's strongest muscle (in the jaw), and a mouthful of friends, there's not much that I can't demolish. I am built in three layers. First is a tough, white outer casing called enamel. Then comes a filler called dentine, and finally pulp.

The mouth is home to Bacterium, whose waste products eat away at my enamel. I should feel no pain because all my nerves are buried deep down, but if Bacterium breaks in, I'll ache for sure. I come in four shapes. Nippers called incisors live at the front. Then come canines—fangs for stabbing food. The wide ones on each side are premolars and molars—they grind food into a paste. The largest molars at the back are "wisdom" teeth, and they don't grow until you are a grown-up yourself.

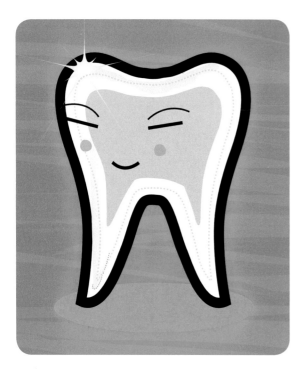

■ Torque

I get things all twisted up. Force normally pushes in one direction, but when it starts turning in a circle, that's when I step in. I am the turning effect of Force—how much of it turns your head.

■ Total Internal Reflection

Refraction and Reflection join at my hip. If Light's beam arrives at the edge of Medium at a sharp angle, it cannot flex its direction and shine through. Instead it reflects off the inside edge and heads back into Medium. Eventually it will arrive at an edge almost straight on, and that's when it will shine through. Diamonds are cut to make use of my effects, so Light twinkles out of the top.

▷ Touch

Give me a hug, I'm the forgotten sense. I'm at work on every inch of your body, and still I get overlooked. But I have so many skills—I can feel hot and cold and a whole  range of pushes, pinches, and pinpricks. I'm right under your skin, where the nerves are plugged into sensors. My system also tells Brain how your body is positioned, so you don't have to think about it.

■ Trachea

You might know me better as windpipe, but I'm the route from mouth and nostril to Lung —and back again. Breathe in, breathe out. Just leave it to me.

T

■ Transformer

Nikola Tesla's great contribution to the modern world, I don't look as exciting as I should really. Maybe that is why I stay out of sight in Electricity's substations. Actually, who am I kidding? It's because I'm very dangerous. Keep out! I'm a ring of solid Iron with close-fitting, figure-hugging coils of Copper's wire. It is my job to change—or transform—Electric Current's voltage. I step up to high Voltage for sending Power long distances, and then step it down to make Electric Current safe to use in houses.

▷ Transistor

Some versions of me control Electric Current's flow, others switch it on or off. I use Semiconductor to turn the current on and off, and I do this thousands of times a second. Computer scientists

arrange me in little teams of two and three to make "logic gates." Each gate turns digital inputs arriving as 1s and 0s (ons and offs) into the correct outputs according to Computer's program. This is how Microchip works.

■ Transparent

You've always been able to see through me! I refer to the way Light can pass right through some materials, like Air and Water.

■ Transpiration

Plants use me to pull Water up tall Stem. I release water vapor from Leaf, and so Osmosis keeps pulling fresh Water into Root.

■ Tremor

I'm the little cousin of Earthquake. My wobbles and shimmies are too weak to wreck much, but don't ignore me. I'm the only warning you'll get of worse to come.

▽ Triangle

A polygon with three vertices and three straight sides, I am a favorite with engineers because of my strength. You'll find me reinforcing skyscrapers, bridges, and dams. My most regular form is equilateral, with all sides the same length and a 60° angle in each corner. Scalene triangles are the exact opposite, with no equal angles or same-length sides. Isosceles triangles manage to have two sides the same and two equal angles, while right-angled triangles famously have one 90°-angle corner.

T

■ Triple Bond

Carbon is good at making connections, but sometimes there are not enough other elements to link to. I'm there to ease Carbon's loneliness by letting two of its atoms bond to each other three times! My links are weak, so molecules that use me tend to explode!

■ Tumor

Always bad news, I'm a growth in the body caused when Cell goes wrong. If I get out of control, I cause cancer. Kill me!

▷ Tundra

Ice cool, I am the world's coldest biome. You can find me in Arctic and alpine areas (high above the timberline). Very little can grow, because high winds and chilly Temperature mean any trees that are bold enough to try are forced to grow along the ground, not stand up straight. The soil is frozen solid for most of the year. This makes the growing season a mere 50 to 60 days each year.

▷ Tungsten

I'm one tough cookie, with the highest melting point of all metals and a boiling point of about 10,000°F (5,500°C). You'll find me hard to liquefy and boil. In fact, you'll find me just plain harder than nails! As the toughest of the tough, I protect soldiers in bulletproof armor plating, but I still manage to bring Light to the world in the filaments of bright and hot light bulbs.

▷ Turbine

I go with the flow and it gets me in a spin. It's my job to turn straight line Motion into rotation. I may be a waterwheel, a windmill, or even a jet engine, but I always work in the same way. A spin is just so much more useful—it turns Wheel and propellers and puts Power into Electricity Generator.

■ Typhoon

I mean "big wind" in Chinese, and I'm the name Hurricane goes by when it swirls into life in the western Pacific and Indian Oceans. Australians call me "cyclone."

T

U

V

W

Ultrasound

What's that you say? I can't hear you—and you cannot hear me either. I'm Sound when Frequency is too high for Ear to detect. I'm used in medical scanning, bouncing my silent echoes off soft Tissue in the body.

▷ Ultraviolet

I am Radiation for Sun worshippers. A little of me is a good thing. I lift the clouds and cheer you up if you're feeling down, but a little too much and I start to annoy the DNA in Skin. I break chemical bonds, unleashing reactive molecules that can cause cancers.

▷ Uncertainty Principle

I'm a certain lack of certainty built into the basic level of Matter and Physics.

At any point in time, you can know where Particle is, but not where it's going. At least I think that's how it works—I'm fuzzy on the details! My vagueness has nothing to do with the difficulty of measuring tiny Quantum things. It has much more to do with how Quantum's particles are also wavy. This wobbliness is described using mathematics. It does not give one simple answer to a question, but several options instead.

Universal Expansion

Universe is everywhere, all the time. That makes sense. However, I involve something a bit harder to understand—I'm making more "everywhere" for Universe to be! Like a bubble of Space-Time, I'm swelling up in all directions. I'm everywhere and getting bigger. But all of space is inside me, so where am I getting all the new space from? That is a question that still needs an answer.

▷ Universal Indicator

Check out that Solution! I'll reveal its pH. I indicate the score with a change of color: red for Acid, green for neutral, and purple for Alkali.

Universe

I am everything you can imagine—and perhaps some things too strange for anyone to have thought of yet. I contain every galaxy, nebula, and star, plus their solar systems. I'm studied by astronomers, who think I was made in a flash 13.8 billion years ago. I've been growing ever since and am at least 93 billion light-years across.

▽ Uranium

I am a powerful fellow. Fire Neutron at one of my isotopes (atomic number 235), and Nucleus splits with a roar of Energy, sending Neutron in all directions and triggering Chain Reaction's move to rip me apart! Control this reaction (called nuclear fission) and I generate Power, but pack me in a bomb and I can flatten whole cities.

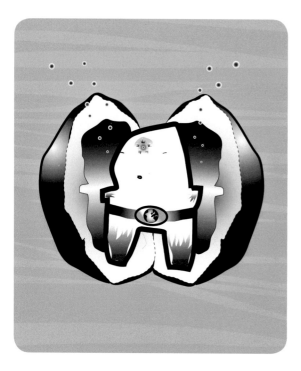

▷ Uranus

I'm the third-largest planet, and I've taken a few knocks in my life. Early on in my history, a humongous collision knocked me over. I now spin on my side, with Axis at right angles to all the other planets. I have a ring system. However, my set of 11 rings is very thin and wasn't spotted until I was photographed by the Kuiper Telescope in 1977.

▷ Urine

I'm a warm, bright, and very wet fellow who cleans you out several times a day. I'm a yellow liquid wrung out from Blood by Kidney when taking away toxins and the unwanted leftovers of metabolism. My main ingredient is urea, a nitrogen-rich Compound made by Liver as it processes Protein in food. It's a poison, so I mix it with Water to make it safe.

Uterus

Also known as a womb, I'm the first home you ever knew. I'm a safe haven inside a mother where you and all other babies develop. While I kept you safe and warm as you grew large and strong enough to take care of yourself, Placenta kept you supplied with Oxygen and food. Once ready, I grew impatient with you and my muscular walls pushed you out! Happy birthday!

U
V
W

▷ **Vaccine**

I'll beef up a body's defenses to diseases by giving Immune System the chance to practice on a lower-strength bad guy. I can be an inactivated bug (like flu) or a live but weakened one (like my TB tackler). I have punted smallpox into the past and almost have polio licked. I also help target cholera, ebola, measles, mumps, rubella, rabies . . .

■ **Vacuole**

A wet and soggy storage bag, I'm a feature of Plant Cell, where I hold spare Starch and other useful chemicals.

▷ **Vacuum**

I am what I am not: a blank space with hardly a crumb of Matter. But can nothing be something? It's only away from the influence of Mass that I near perfection.

I don't exert Friction on objects passing through me. Light also travels at its fastest.

I clean your home, pack food for freshness, and keep drinks hot or cold in thermoses. But step outside a spacecraft in outer space and I'll suck the life out of you in less than a minute. Yet even in the emptiness there's a flicker of restlessness: Dark Energy. You might get something from nothing after all!

▽ **Vein**

I'm your body's aristocrat—a true blue-blooded grandee. I run Circulatory System's home stretch, bringing woozy Blood back to Heart. That dude's oxygen-carrying journey is over for the time being, and who can blame it for having the blues? (In fact, it may be called blue, but the oxygen-poor blood I carry is actually a dull red color.) I may not have Artery's heart-felt pressure, but my one-way valves stop exhausted Blood from slipping back down the tube!

■ **Velocity**

You should turn to pace-setting Speed to get the basic idea, but I give one important extra detail. My measure always includes direction, which is essential when figuring out Relative Speed.

▷ Venus

Bright and shiny, I hang in the night sky, a dazzling beauty.

My starlike brilliance is caused by Sun's rays being reflected from my thick clouds—this makes me the most radiant object in the night sky after the Moon. I am named after the Roman goddess of love and appear just before sunrise or just after sunset, so you may also know me as the morning or evening star.

▷ Vertebrate

Defined as having a backbone, I belong to a group that makes up just a tiny fraction of animal life. Still, my clan includes the biggest animals of all—and humans!

▷ Virus

I'm a death-dealing devil and real bad news for all other living things. Sometimes I'm just a nuisance, causing a cold or chickenpox, but I can also be deadly. My dangerous forms include ebola and HIV. I'm a tiny DNA bandit and couldn't be simpler; I barely count as a living thing. I don't eat or grow, but I hijack Cell and make it my slave.

■ Visceral Cavity

I'll have your guts and most of your other internal organs, too. I'm the space inside the body of Vertebrate and other complex animals where innards are packed in for safekeeping. I am a blind, airless, and bloodless bag with no way in or out. It's always best if you keep me that way.

▽ Vision

I have the power. The power of sight. Animals use different eye designs to make me work, but I'm always based on a chemical change occurring in Eye's pigment cells that is triggered by Energy delivered by Photon. I'll add color by detecting Light's wavelength using special cone-shaped cells. Then it is Brain's job to transform the pattern in Light's beam into a mental image.

U
V
W

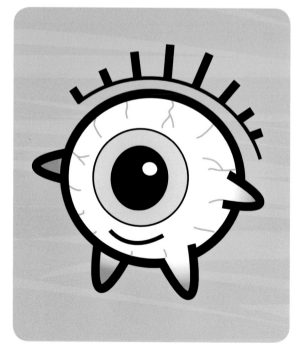

▽ Volcano

When I'm in a foul mood, it's time for the scientists to leave the area and let all their probing gizmos monitor Temperature. I'm deadly—my poisonous smell alone can kill.

Some say I'm like a big zit. Well, yeah, I do break out on Earth's surface, fill up with angry liquid, and grow until I erupt. I'm famous for spewing oozy Lava, erupting sky—high with columns of ash, throwing boiling clouds of dust and mud down my sides, and chucking out a medley of Ejecta's rock bombs. When I'm feeling menacing, I can blow my top. I'm most likely to appear in places where tectonic plates meet. I had my heyday four billion years ago, when I played a big friendly part in cooling the molten planet. I released Gas back, and it was this that formed early Atmosphere.

■ Volt

I'm a measure of the forcer pushing Electric Current. I'm named after Alessandro Volta, the Italian inventor of the battery.

▷ Volume

Nobody's as good at taking up space as I am! My interest lies in how much space something takes up or the amount of liquid or gas it would hold if it were hollow— I'm talking capacity.

I rely on three dimensions to find out—length, height, and depth.

■ Warm-Blooded

Most mammals and birds make lots of Heat inside their body to keep themselves warm. Cold-blooded creatures, such as Reptile, need a sunny spot to warm up.

▷ Water

I am the most essential substance on this planet. Life as we know it is simply not possible without me. I make up 70 percent of you. My most common form on Earth is as Liquid,

flowing in River and filling up Crust's low points as Lake and Ocean. As Solid, I am cold ice, a brittle crystal that caps Earth's poles. I also exist as an invisible gaseous vapor, which fills up Atmosphere with billowing clouds.

Water Bear

Don't be fooled by my cute and cuddly name; I'm a grizzly old soldier. I'm built like a tank with my hard outer shell. I can cling on to Life just one degree above Absolute Zero. Brrr! Put me in a frying pan and I'll grin and bear it—Temperature can hit 300°F (150°C), before I even flinch. I can survive ten years without "essential" Water. When times are tough, I go into suspended animation.

▽ Water Cycle

Stuck on repeat, I have no beginning and no end. With the limited amount of water on Earth, I've got no choice but to stay on a permanent loop. At my heart are three processes. Evaporation sends water vapor into Air. Condensation cools this vapor into clouds of droplets. Then Precipitation splish-splashes rain back to the surface.

Watt

The unit of Power, I was named after James Watt, the Scot who built powerful engines. One watt (1W) equals 1 joule per second.

▷ Wave

Aloha! I'm a thrill-seeking surfer dude who always rocks the boat. I'm a way for Energy to get around. I only move up and down, like a person in a crowd doing the wave. No one in the crowd actually moves seats, but the wave (and Energy) does. The more Energy I carry, the higher my peaks and deeper the troughs.

Wavelength

Along with Frequency, I'm the primary measure of Wave—the length from one peak to the next, my size really matters.

▷ Weak Force

I have to be honest with you, I'm a little upset to be known as the weak force. I'm no weakling—I'm over a trillion trillion times stronger than Gravity! But compared to Strong Force, well, you get it, I'm weak. I battle with Nucleon in Atom's nucleus. It's me reorganizing Proton and Neutron during Fusion, Fission, and Radioactive Decay.

U
V
W

▷ Wedge

As sharp as ever, I look like Ramp on its side, with one wide end (push here) and one narrow end (don't touch!). As a Stone-Age cutter, I'm the oldest machine of all.

▽ Weight

People who check their weight are actually interested in Mass. Mass tells you how much Matter is in an object, whereas I tell you only what force it exerts (what "push" it has) when pulled down by Gravity. You can use me to measure Mass, too. If something weighs ten times as much as another thing, it has ten times as much Mass. Heavy stuff!

▷ Wheel and Axle

Let's start this thing a-rollin'! We are the winning combo that gets people on the move. Anything that uses a disk shape to trundle along sets our unique skills in motion.

Sure, Wheel does all the work, but it would be useless without sturdy Axle connecting that dizzy disk to the mechanism. Most axles sit dead-center, allowing Wheel to spin around freely.

■ Whisker

A handsome addition to any face, I am really there for when there is nothing to see—when it's too dark. I am stiff Hair that pokes out from an animal's face, with lots of us mapping out a space the size of the head. If one of us touches something, we sound a warning. We're ideal for finding safe spaces when Vision cannot be relied upon.

▷ White Blood Cell

I belong to an elite bloodstream unit pledged "to serve and protect." We seek and destroy evildoers like germs, cancer and Virus. Neutrophils target enemy bacteria;

basophils trigger allergic-response chemicals. Eosinophils stalk Parasite, and monocytes mop up debris. Heading up the crew are lymphocytes, which kill cells gone bad.

U
V
W

▷ White Dwarf

I'm what is left once Star has given its all. After Red Giant has finally given up the Fusion game, I am all that remains. I am its hot core left behind. I'm about the size of Earth and am destined to gradually cool and fade as my nuclear fires have shut down. That will take tens of billions of years. But one day I'll be too cold to see—an invisible Black Dwarf.

■ WIMP

Weakly Interacting Massive Particles, I am a possible answer to Dark Matter. If found, I'd have Weight but would do almost nothing.

▷ Wireless

Look, no wires! With my incomprehensible powers, I allow electronic devices to talk to each other with no physical connection. Spooky, huh? Not really—your machine just needs a built-in wireless adapter to make it happen. I use Radio Wave to send messages to a base station as Wi-Fi. This wireless access point provides a gateway to the Internet, through which any wireless-enabled gizmo can enter.

Meanwhile, bluetooth (named after Harald, a Danish king) unites electronic devices, allowing them to share info—swapping files on two cell phones, for example. Unfortunately, microwave ovens and cordless telephones use the same Frequency and can sometimes cause interference. Ring, ring. Ping!

■ Woodland

My friend Forest has an unbroken layer of leaves in the treetops, whereas I'm thin enough on top to let a lot of Light in.

■ Work

According to physicists, I am whenever Force transfers Energy to Mass.

▷ Worm

I am happy to live almost anywhere. With no backbone for support, I grow largest in Water, but I also wriggle through soil, of course—and in Intestines, too!

U

V

W

X Y Z

■ X and Y Chromosomes

A mismatched pair, we get to decide who's Male and Female. Male gets an X paired with tiny Y, while Female always gets the double X.

▷ X-Ray

A star with that all-important "X" factor, I'm made when streams of high-energy Electron slam into Metal. My most famous use is in hospitals, where I look for broken Bone.

I zap straight through soft Tissue, but not Bone, so it shows up as ghostly Skeleton on photographic paper.

■ Xylem

I ring hollow because I'm a network of tubes that run from Root through Leaf to Stem. I'm a plant's water supply system, and once I reach the end of my usefulness, I can be toughened up to make wood.

■ Year

Once around Sun, that's all it takes. I am the longest tick and tock of Earth's time system. I'm 365 days long because that is the time it takes for Planet Earth to circle Sun.

▷ Yeast

Hic! I'm a gassy geezer who puts the bubbles into beer and makes bread rise to the occasion. Naturally occurring, I'm commonly found on the skins of grapes.

When grapes are crushed, I begin to feast on the sugary pulp, turning the juice fizzy and alcoholic. When I am added to bread dough, I make bubbles of Carbon Dioxide, which fluff up the loaf. I'm also a model organism for genetic research, for use in microbial Fuel Cell, and as a producer of Biofuel. Please, it's the "yeast" I can do!

■ Yield

I'm a word with more than one meaning, but in science I am all about results. In Chemical Reaction, I'm the measure of how much Reactant has turned into Product. Chemical engineers look for ways to give me a boost.

■ Yolk

Babies are always hungry, and I'm a perfect meal for Embryo, ready and waiting in Egg.

▷ Zero

I am something that stands for nothing. You know my sign, the round mark. Be warned! I have extraordinary powers. Put my digit at the end of a number and I make the number ten times larger. And then there's the curse of zero. Divide by me and your calculator will return a big fat ERROR! Multiply by me and any number—no matter how large—vanishes, reduced to . . . well, zero.

▷ Zinc

Here to protect and serve, I'm more useful than you'd ever *zinc*! I'm a very sociable Element who's always happy to mix in with other metals. Brass is probably my best-known Alloy, formed when I get together with Copper. I'm a little reactive when left alone but can be found in batteries.

With a thin layer of my atoms I "galvanize" Steel, stopping Water and Oxygen from rusting it away. Even if I am scratched and Steel becomes exposed, I quickly form zinc oxide before any Iron in Steel has a chance to corrode. I also protect people from sunburn as the white zinc oxide sunblock that's ever-popular with cricketers. What's more, I'm an essential element for loads of body processes and I can be taken as a dietary supplement.

■ Zoology

I'm going to the zoo, how about you, and you and you? Please come, because that is what I am all about. I am the study of animals, from the shuffling slime of placozoa and simple sponge to the great complexity of dolphin and (ahem) human beings. My scientists also figure out which animals live together, and how they behave and breed.

■ Zygote

In the beginning there was me. Sperm and Egg merge, and two become one. I am the first cell of a new Organism. I have a full set of chromosomes and all the organelles I need. To grow a new body, I'll need to divide, and divide again—maybe trillions of times. I am also Stem Cell, and so can develop into anything the body needs.

X
Y
Z

Pythagoras

The Greek mathematician behind the right-angle triangle theorem.

Archimedes

This Greek gadget geek devised the lever, screw, and pulley.

Eratosthenes

A Greek mathematician, and the first to measure Earth's size.

Galileo Galilei

An Italian astronomer who was the first to see stars with a telescope.

Charles Lyell

A Scotsman heralded as the grandfather of geology.

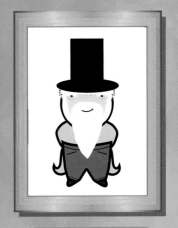

Charles Darwin

An English biologist with big ideas about evolution.

■ Hall of Fame: Great Scientists

Science does not happen by itself, you know. It needs scientists to use theories and experiments to figure it all out. The job of a scientist sounds a lot of fun because you are allowed to get it wrong—in fact, being wrong is another way of learning what's right. However, it has to be said we remember the ones who got it right, such as this gang of greats, more than those that did not. Between them they've explained how everything works, from A to Z.

Dmitri Mendeleev

The Russian chemist who invented the periodic table of elements.

Antonie van Leeuwenhoek
This Dutchman invented what we now call a microscope.

Isaac Newton
The English scientist behind the principles of modern physics.

Antoine Lavoisier
This French father of chemistry named oxygen and hydrogen.

Ada Lovelace
An English mathematician and the first computer programmer.

Marie Curie
This Polish-born scientist led research into radioactivity.

Albert Einstein
A German-born scientist obsessed with space, time, mass, and energy.

Craig Venter
This American is one of today's leading genetic engineers.

Erwin Schrödinger
An Austrian physicist and early adopter of quantum physics.

Index

Index

Index